An Odyssey of Joy

Truth for Today

An Odyssey of Joy

THE MESSAGE OF PHILIPPIANS

Sam Gordon

BELFAST, NORTHERN IRELAND
GREENVILLE, SOUTH CAROLINA

AN ODYSSEY OF JOY
© 2004 Sam Gordon

All rights reserved

ISBN 1 84030 155 4

Ambassador Publications
a division of
Ambassador Productions Ltd.
Providence House
Ardenlee Street
Belfast
BT6 8QJ
Northern Ireland
www.ambassador-productions.com

Emerald House
427 Wade Hampton Blvd.
Greenville
SC 29609, USA
www.emeraldhouse.com

Trans World Radio
Southstoke Lane
BATH
BA2 5SH
United Kingdom

01225 831390

www.twr.org.uk

Trans World Radio
P O Box 8700
Cary
NC 27512, USA

1 800 456 7TWR

www.twr.org

DEDICATION

to

Lois

*my darling wife in
a life of joyous fulfilment*

Truth for Today

~ Mission Statement ~

*'To teach the entire Bible in a warm expository
style so that people's lives are influenced to such
a degree that they impact their world for Christ.'*

First Word

'Joy is the serious business of heaven,' wrote C S Lewis.

We strike gold when we discover that spiritual euphoria is also the surprising theme of Paul's letter to the church at Philippi. It is even more incredible when we realise that Paul was not living in a five star luxury suite in the local Crowne Plaza hotel. Rather, he said what he had to say from the cramped and sparsely furnished apartment he rented downtown Rome.

Paul was deprived of his freedom. He was under house arrest and chained to a big, burly Roman soldier, 24/7. Times were tough. Really tough. He was a political prisoner facing possible execution. He had no mission board supporting him and no legal aid society defending him. His back was to the wall. He was tumbling from crisis to crisis.

And yet, when the winsomely human Paul picked up his quill and wrote on the parchment, he penned an upbeat letter—a letter that resonates with joy—for joy is the exuberant buoyancy of a confidence that is deeply rooted in God. We hear his chains chiming like Christmas bells!

That means when the bubble of your life is about to burst, when you are beginning to ping under relentless pressure, when it seems as though your get up and go has done just that and got up and gone, when rolling out of bed is tougher than jumping into bed, when you are pulling your hair out and screaming at the kids—you need to call a time-out—you need a margin to bounce back.

You can be joyful, even though you are a Christian!

Sam Gordon

Contents

1
No people like God's people

'From there we travelled to Philippi …' (Acts 16:12)

Seems pretty obvious. But getting there was not that simple. Life rarely is. There were many moments of deep uncertainty. There were times when Paul must have wondered: 'Is this really happening to me?' He persistently knocked on a number of doors—Asia and Bithynia. All stayed shut. It was no, no, no! A series of dead ends. Every possibility was vetoed by the sovereign Spirit of God. They were for another time and perhaps for other people.

Bless Paul's heart, he was caught between a rock and a hard place. He had itchy feet. He sensed it was time to move on even though God was blessing his gospel preaching with many outstanding headline conversions. The Christians were being strengthened in their faith and churches were mushrooming and growing daily. The apostle was living on the crest of a wave. The evangelical flame was spreading. Fast. Exciting times.

In his heart, however, Paul knew that the God of the Great Commission had other ideas up his sleeve.

True enough. Paul found himself in Troas, just ten miles down the road from the famous city of Troy, on the west coast of Asia Minor. He settled down for the night. It had been an incredibly long day. In the wee small hours he had a vision where he saw a man from Macedonia pleading 'come over [here] and help us' (Acts 16:9). It is worth noting that Macedonia had been the power base for the conquest of the then known world by the most famous Macedonian of them all—Alexander the Great.

Be that as it may, Paul felt this was it. Great! The impasse had been resolved. At that moment, Paul discovered that God's 'no' was just as important as God's 'go'. This was the green light for which he had been waiting. He knew it and, without a moment's hesitation, off he went to live the dream.

Europe ... here we come!

After the 125-mile sea trip—north west—the group arrived at the port of Neapolis (modern Kavalla) and, when they stepped ashore, the East was behind them and the West stretched before them. Paul and his entourage then travelled some 10 miles west to Philippi (*cf.* Acts 16:11, 12) in what has been called 'the greatest event in history.' For the best part of four millennia, Asia had been the cradle of the human race. Now that centre was moving to Europe.

Let me back up for a moment: at Neapolis, the great *Via Egnatia*, a military road and a critical artery of commerce which the Romans built to link Europe and Asia, the Adriatic with the Aegean and the Bosphorus, met the sea, after passing through the city centre of Philippi.

Sooner or later all four of them—Paul, Silas, Timothy, and Luke—arrived in the city whose Greek name means 'lover of horses'. What a fantastic welcome they received. You must be joking! No one knew they were coming. There was no tourist information office so they had to find their own way around town and be content with doing their own thing. This was new territory. These guys were pioneers on virgin soil.

However, '... the assault of the gospel of Christ upon the power, culture, and corruption of Greek civilisation had begun in earnest.' (J A Motyer)

Postcard on Philippi

It is estimated at that time the population of Philippi, one of the region's premier cities, was fairly close to 15,000 people. It was probably two-thirds Greek and one-third Roman, the Romans being the descendants of the original veteran colonists and of Italian stock. By the time Paul rolled into town, the grandchildren of the soldiers who had helped Octavian win the mastery of the world were middle-aged. These were augmented by freed slaves.

The more numerous Greeks were either native or immigrants, only a few of whom would have been granted Roman citizenship. The reality is, the Greeks were in a majority of two to one, but the Romans were in power. It was, as it were, Rome in microcosm—there were Roman houses, Roman officials, Roman soldiers, Roman togas, Roman speech, and Roman merchants. As Philip Greenslade indicates: 'This is reflected in the fact that virtually all the inscriptions excavated at the site have been in Latin.'

Today the ancient city of Philippi lies as an assortment of melancholy ruins—having said that, it is well worth a visit if you happen to be in the region and passing through the modern city of Filippoi. If you are really keen, there is also a museum with fine artefacts at Kavalla.

The site has been carefully excavated by archaeologists who have uncovered a marketplace, the foundation of a large arched gateway, a temple built to the honour of the Roman god Silvanus, and an amphitheatre dating back to Roman times.

Down by the riverside

So what did the foursome do? What was their strategy? They kept their heads down for a few days and then, on the Saturday, they searched high and low for a synagogue. They looked in vain. There wasn't one! Reason: ten Jewish men were needed to form the quorum or *minyan* required to constitute such a gathering. Such was the real world of Philippi.

The reality hit home but, in all fairness to them, they did not give up. Not that easily! They wended their way down by the deep, swift-flowing stream known as the Gangites 'where [they] expected to find a place of prayer' (Acts 16:13). Their journey was fruitful as a number of religiously inclined women had taken quality time out to seek the God of Abraham, Isaac, and Jacob.

It seems that Paul wasted no time in getting down to brass tacks. He pulled no punches in sharing with them the story of God's redeeming love. As he ministered the word of God to them, the Spirit of God was doing what he does best—he was actively working in the life of one of the ladies. The biographer Luke says of Lydia that 'the Lord opened her heart to respond to Paul's message' (Acts 16:14). An inner lamp was switched on.

The first convert in Philippi was a Gentile lady—an Asian on business in Europe.

From an acorn to an oak tree

Thank God, that was only the start. Unpretentious maybe. At least the ball was rolling. Within hours, it picked up speed and gathered momentum for many others were transformed by the life-changing power of the gospel of Christ. Dr Luke's record in Acts 16 is a fascinating account of God at work. In no time at all a church—the original Riverside Evangelical Church—was born in the place of prayer.

Ten years later, around AD 62, Paul dropped them a line that incites them and us to love God more. On a few sheets of stiff, scratchy paper he wrote them an inspirational letter full of warm, personal spiritual nourishment on how to be an up person in a down world. Heart to heart. Short and sweet. Magnificent though brief. A wee gem that sparkles with truth. A priceless parchment.

It is a delectably delicious piece of mail that contains only 104 verses—at most, a twelve or thirteen minute read from start to finish. And because the message is so captivating and scintillating, it leaves us gasping for breath. A good read.

Supremely it is all about joy. A journey into joy. Actually the Greek word for joy, in both its noun and verb forms, appears more than a dozen times in its four chapters (*cf.* 1:4, 18, 25; 2:2, 17, 18, 28, 29; 3:1; 4:1, 4, 10). R C H Lenski wrote: 'Joy is the music that runs through this epistle, the sunshine that spreads over all of it.'

Reading it cover to cover makes me feel like the playboy who, after he was saved, stood up in church and shared his testimony in his own inimitable way: 'I am happier now when I'm not happy than I was before when I was happy!' To quote Billy Sunday: 'If there is no joy in your religion, there is a leak in your Christianity somewhere!'

The epistle to the Philippians is like a breath of fresh air. It is like walking into a room that is filled with the fragrant scent of beautiful roses. It pulsates and radiates joy. Compared with some of Paul's other epistles, this one oozes joy. For example, the folks in Corinth left him feeling rather discouraged, the people in Galatia depressed him, but these good friends have a hugely positive influence on Paul, they leave him delighted.

Philippians—God wrote it. Paul just held the quill.

A good laugh

An easy to remember outline favoured by Charles Swindoll is:

* there is laughter in living (chapter one),
* there is laughter in serving (chapter two),
* there is laughter in sharing (chapter three), and
* there is laughter in resting (chapter four).

1:1

A dynamic duo

Paul and Timothy. What a way to commence a letter. It certainly would not happen today. It is not what we find in the average third millennium textbook, except that it was the norm in the first century. Paul signed his name at the beginning of the letter rather than burying it at the end. In the opening sentence, he told them who he was.

Can you imagine the scene? It was Sunday morning in the church at Philippi, a church dubbed as Paul's 'sweetheart' church. One of the elders stood before the assembled congregation to tell them what was happening the following week, and to read them a letter. He told them it was from a long lost friend. The people were sitting in suspense, on tenterhooks, wondering. Who? Then, with emotion in his voice, he dropped the name: *Paul.* Definitely not a clanger.

That was all they needed—a kaleidoscope of memories flooded back, the smiles appeared, the eyes filled up with a few tears, their ears cocked— you could hear a pin drop, the mere mention of his name sent a shiver down their spines and legs turned to jelly.

* Ten years ago this man was among them as an evangelist and church planter.
* Ten years ago he was unceremoniously incarcerated in the local jail as an innocent man.
* Ten years ago they had seen God work in a spectacular manner as people were gloriously converted from all walks of life.

And now—a decade later—his name pops up again. It was almost too good to be true. How it must have thrilled them and warmed the cockles of their hearts.

A blast from the past

'Like art loving Italians thrilled by the works of Michelangelo, like sixteenth-century German believers who were inspired by a spokesman named Martin Luther, like nineteenth-century black Americans who grasped at every word from Abraham Lincoln, like twentieth-century patriotic Britons who needed a Winston Churchill to help them hold fast, the people of the church at Philippi respected and needed Paul. He was their founder and friend. He was their teacher, their able and much admired leader.' (Charles Swindoll)

This was no one-man show on a one-night stand. Paul was not in the business of empire building nor was he interested in starting his own denomination. He also included Timothy—half Jew, half Gentile, wholly Christian—in his initial greeting to the church. Apart from the fact that he was his son in the faith, a protégé, and a cherished companion, he also played a major role in Paul's evangelistic outreach. He was a valued member of the team. The folks at Philippi would know him and love him. Unknown to them, however, very shortly he would be paying them another visit as the personal emissary of the apostle.

Paul (*Paulos*) and Timothy (*Timotheos*) were a formidable team. They had their individual strengths and weaknesses and, because of that, they beautifully complemented one another. Each one had a vital job to do and a unique contribution to make. Neither felt threatened. They had their problems, their bones of contention, sure they did, but they worked them through and came out stronger and still smiling. By all accounts, they were the best of friends and an excellent partnership.

Big name or plain Mr Paul

- He was the prince of preachers.
- He was the man who blazed a trail for God in pagan, inky black darkness.
- He was a missionary to the regions beyond.
- He took the gospel where man had never taken it before.
- He held city wide crusades.
- He planted scores of churches.
- He was prolific with his pen.
- He was in great demand across Asia, Europe, and the Middle East.

The people then had the mindset which said:

---

why go for skimmed milk when we can enjoy real cream?

How did Paul introduce himself? As a *servant (doulos) of Christ (Christos) Jesus (Iēsous)*. Wow! What prodigious humility. He was all of this and more, yet he saw himself as a slave. A bondslave (*cf.* Exodus 21:5, 6). Based on the Old Testament analogy, Paul is intensely loyal to Jesus because he really loved his Lord and Saviour. He is totally committed to him with one hundred percent allegiance. The Lord owns him lock, stock, and barrel.

In the 'caste system' world of his day, to be labelled a *servant* meant you had no personal rights, you were nothing more than chattel. For instance, if you worked for a farmer, you were listed on his inventory as a 'speaking tool' to distinguish you from animals which were classified as 'dumb tools'.

Often times it was an extremely harsh existence of vilification and horrendous abuse—verbal, physical, mental, and emotional. Well documented examples abound of cases where, for example, servants who broke a wine glass were fed to piranha fish, and so on.

What you see is what you get

Nothing reveals more about how Paul saw himself after his conversion than the way he frequently identified himself. You can usually tell what kind of a man you are dealing with by the way he introduces himself. Paul has no delusions of grandeur. No airs or graces. He is transparent. He did not say:

- 'Hi folks! I'm Paul ... the pedigreed former bigwig in the antichristian Gestapo.'
- 'Hi folks! I'm Paul ... the guy with the sensational it's-never-happened-this-way-before conversion experience.'
- 'Hi folks! I'm Paul ... the famous you-must-have-heard-of-me apostle to the G ntiles.'
- 'Hi folks! I'm P ul ... the never-short-of-something-to-say author of most of the New Testament epistles.'

However, the preacher man did say: 'Hi folks! I'm Paul, a servant of Christ Jesus'—period. Humble, yes. Genuine, yes. But there is also the mark of true greatness. Paul discovered perfect freedom in willing service. The lesson is clear: we can be too big for God to use but never too small. For the man who is all wrapped up in himself is overdressed.

Wee man, big God

Paul did not act like a prima donna who had to be worshipped, or a fragile hero who had to be treated with kid gloves. He saw himself as a servant. The Latin *paulus* means 'little' or 'small'. No doubt about it, he certainly lived up to his name.

Paul was not interested in doing the evangelical circuit as a celebrity, keynote speaker. He did not run around the country or cross continents holding seminars on the *how to* or *how not to* of Christian ministry. He was not a full time worker doing a part time job. Nor was his a luxurious lifestyle with all the attendant paraphernalia. He was only a servant. Having said that, no greater honour or dignity could be conferred upon him.

Why should he stoop to be a cardboard pin-up only as good as his last sermon?

The adulation of an adoring (and fickle) public dies away but the glowing praise of an eternal God lives on for ever. 'We all would do well to remember,' writes David Jeremiah, 'that God did not save us to become sensations, but rather to become servants.'

Down caste

Sadhu Sundar Singh (1889-1929) was born into an Indian family of high caste. When he became a Christian and told his parents of his decision, they said: 'You have broken caste.' They immediately banished him from their home.

It was the wet season, and the rain was coming down hard as he left his home, clad in only his insubstantial Indian robes. He sat under a nearby tree all night, soaked to the skin. He said that he felt so radiantly happy, however, that he forgot any physical discomfort. He had the freedom to travel throughout the region telling the Jesus story.

He became known as the apostle of India. Once he went into Tibet, where he was arrested, put into a pit, and branded with irons. He bore those scars the rest of his life. While speaking in England, he said: 'I am going back to do what I have done. I am quite aware of the cost.' Sometime after his return to India, he disappeared and appears to have suffered a martyr's death.

Sadhu willingly moved from being high caste in India to that of a servant—one of God's untouchables.

Icons in pews

Paul's insightful letter is specifically addressed to *all the saints (hagios) in Christ Jesus at Philippi (Philippoi)*. These were no alabaster gurus sitting on a gilt pedestal. We will not find them cast in marble nor will we see them set in decorative stained glass in some Gothic cathedral window. They are not a cluster of 'do not touch' highly polished statues sitting in an ornate museum.

They are saints. Ordinary people—very ordinary people—who know Jesus personally. The title baggage had nothing to do with them. It is not their fault that they are branded in this way. It is the living God who has set them apart for himself. He is the one who, in grace, seized the initiative and titled them because he had a special purpose for them. As saints, they are his exclusive people. And so are we.

They have not been canonised by Rome, but they have been cleansed by precious blood. And claimed. They are not super-pious, elitist individuals who are paid up members of a Christian country club. They are everyday, plain vanilla people made of the same material as the rest of us. The fact is there are only two categories of people in the world: the saints and the aints!

Location, location, location

And, on top of that, they are *in* Christ Jesus. A Buddhist does not speak of himself as *in* Buddha, nor does a follower of Islam speak of himself as *in* Mohammed. A Christian Scientist is not *in* Mary Baker Eddy, nor a Mormon *in* Joseph Smith or Brigham Young. Individuals of that persuasion may faithfully embrace and follow the teaching and example of those now deceased religious or cult leaders, but they are not *in* them.

That is where God's people are unique—remarkably unique—for they alone can claim to be *in* their living Lord and Saviour, Jesus Christ. It is *in* him that we enjoy the benefits and blessings of a full and free salvation.

No matter what happens to us in this life, Jesus is our permanent address! He is our zip code.

Servants and *saints* is the registered trademark of the people of God. Both reveal to us the distinguishing marks of the real Christian. 'Great though our privileges are, they are not to be equated with dressing gown and slippers,' writes J A Motyer, 'they are staff and shoes for pilgrimage, armour for battle, and a plough for the field.'

You see, the *saint in Christ Jesus* is also a *servant of Christ Jesus*. Obedience is the name of the game. It is Jesus who has made all the difference. It is only by grace—amazing grace—that they are *in* Christ and in the church at all. In his ineffable light and before his awesome presence, social status is turned upside down.

- Measured by him, we are all servants.
- Measured by what we are in him, we are all saints.

Meet the leaders

Paul introduces us to the leadership in the local church when he speaks of *the overseers (episkopos) and deacons (diakonos)*. The former are primarily responsible for the spiritual wellbeing of the fellowship and the latter take care of the material needs within the company of believers.

Their essential ministry and character qualifications are clearly spelled out in 1 Timothy 3:1-13 and Titus 1:6-9. The major difference between the two roles is that the elders are to be skilled in teaching biblical truth.

The leadership team was not an imposition on the church fellowship but an extension of it. Joe and Mary and everyone else in the church are not 'under' them per se, but *with* them. Here is the distinctive nature of the local church. This is what constitutes a New Testament church:

- it is comprised of saints,
- ruled by godly elders, and
- served by faithful deacons.

There is no top down hierarchy as such. Having said that, there is an organised structure—there has to be if things are going to run smoothly. When it comes to leadership in the local church it is important to realise we do not start at the bottom and work our way up. It is not a matter of climbing up the ladder to the office of deacon or being promoted to a higher rung upon recognition as an elder/overseer. No, it is not quite like that, at all. It is not tiered in that sense. Our feet remain on level ground even though our responsibilities differ and may increase.

Leadership is service—an opportunity to serve each other.

1:2

Enjoy the blessing

Paul could not have wished anything better for them in his sanctified hello. This was the longing in his heart: that they might know double blessings for we read: *Grace (charis) and peace (eirēnē) to you from God (Theos) our Father (Patēr) and the Lord (Kyrios) Jesus Christ.*

A double-barrelled blessing. The pièces de résistance of a gospel which is Paul's magnificent obsession. We have grace and peace, a compressed message which packs a theological punch. The order is of ultra importance. We can never know peace in our hearts without first experiencing the grace of God. Peace is a wonderful spin-off from the grace of God. From a different perspective, grace is the fountain of which peace is a flowing stream. Or as Ralph Martin says: 'Peace is the fruit of God's gracious activity in the experience of sinners.'

Grace, a sunshine word, is something that comes to us which we do not deserve and which we cannot repay. Grace stoops to where we are and lifts us to where we ought to be. Grace is everything—for nothing— to those who do not deserve anything.

Peace, an azure blue sky word, is something that happens within us— a freedom from inner distraction, an internal rest. Peace is a tranquillity of soul that frees us from fear and takes the sharp edges off our anxiety. It deals with those things that cause us to wobble.

Grace and peace do not come from ourselves, no matter how positive our thoughts, nor do they come from others, no matter how assuring or wise their counsel. They come only from God.

When Paul breathed his blessing on the congregation, it assumed huge significance because of the very public squabble between two leading female lights in the assembly. Their behaviour was upsetting the apple cart and it would take a lot of grace to restore the shattered peace.

John Phillips makes the valid point: 'Where there is grace there can be no commencement of hostilities. Where there is peace there can be no continuation of hostilities. Grace means that war is impossible; peace means that the war is over. Contention only flourishes in the absence of grace and peace.'

He is my everything

After conducting Beethoven's moving and magnificent *Ninth Symphony*, Arturo Toscanini brought down his baton to a burst of spontaneous applause. The appreciative audience roared in rapturous acclaim and approval. Toscanini and his orchestra took repeated bows.

When the cheering finally subsided, Toscanini turned back to his musicians and leaned over the podium. Voicing his words in staccato whispers, he said to the men: 'Gentlemen, I am nothing. And you are nothing. Beethoven is everything, everything, everything!'

Whether it is Toscanini or Paul—whether we are in a cell, a church, or a car—whether we are in Perth, Philadelphia, Peterhead, or Philippi—these people are nothing. We are nothing. Jesus Christ is everything! When that truth is embedded in our minds, we will be satisfied to be the least of saints, the foremost of sinners, used by the Lord.

When the credits roll at the end of the movie of our lives, Jesus takes all the praise.

1:3

Thanks a lot!

Paul's soul is a carillon, and the first bell to be struck is that of thanksgiving. In fact, the first two words say it all: *I thank (eucharisteō)*. Paul was showing a spirit of genuine appreciation for them. It was a note of heartfelt gratitude for their practical fellowship in the gospel, these folks have been so good to him in so many ways. He was not flattering them, he was not trying to butter them up in any way—he was doing nothing more than telling the truth.

There was an affinity that they so obviously enjoyed, the one with the other. A oneness of purpose. A sense of mutual understanding. A bond that bound their hearts together. These guys really hit it off, big time. They clicked.

No wonder Paul wrote: *I thank my God every (pas) time I remember (mneia) you.* The Baptist preacher C H Spurgeon once said that there must be a 'think' at the bottom of 'thank'. He meant that there ought to be intelligent content to our praise. And so, when Paul takes a walk down memory lane, his recollection is such that he just says: 'Thanks, Lord, they're a great bunch of folks!' William Shakespeare wrote: 'O Lord, that lends me life, lend me a heart replete with thankfulness.'

Every time Paul thought of them, they brought a smile to his face. You see, people look different when we pray for them and especially if we thank God for them. Warren Wiersbe suggests that we should all ask ourselves: 'Am I the kind of person who brings joy to my pastor's mind when he thinks of me?'

Don't forget to remember

One of the failures of our lives is how forgetful we are. We are a lot like the couple who were sitting in church when the wife turned to her husband and blurted out: 'O dear, I forgot to turn off the electric iron before we left home!' Her husband looked at her and smiled: 'Don't worry, honey, it won't burn long. I just remembered I forgot to turn off the faucet in the bathroom.' There are some things and some people we should never forget.

'Like a bird singing in the rain, let grateful memories survive in time of sorrow.' (Robert Louis Stevenson)

- Paul had no hangups about his time there.
- He had no regrets.
- He nursed no ill feelings.
- He had no chip on his shoulder.
- He struggled through no unresolved conflicts.

His abiding memories were wonderfully happy ones, they were incredibly positive and, remember, Paul was not looking through rose-tinted spectacles. It is obvious that Paul was made for Philippi and, at the same time, they were good for him. A successful ministry, by any stretch of the imagination. A fruitful relationship like that works two ways, for that is what happens when there is a round peg in a round hole. It is a natural fit. 'The problem with so many preachers,' said the country preacher with his Southern drawl, 'is they has went when they ain't been sent!'

1:4-8

Life ... and lots of it!

Now we know why Paul felt the way he did. The answer is found in the closing phrase in verse 7 where we read: ... *for whether I am in chains (desmos) or defending (apologia) and confirming (bebaiōsis) the gospel (euangelion), all of you share (eimi synkoinōnos) in God's grace with me.* Irrespective of what was happening to Paul a few miles down the road, they had something in common—an enriching experience of the marvellously freeing grace of God.

As individuals, they have been to Calvary, they have been to an empty tomb, they have fallen prostrate before the throne of the exalted and glorified Lamb—that, perhaps more than anything else, is what forged a kindred spirit. At the very heart of their relationship with each other was the conscious realisation that they were but needy sinners saved by the matchless grace of God.

They were beggars sharing the same loaf of bread.

There they were—sharing the same joyous life, bound for the same eternal destination in heaven, and serving the same living Lord Jesus. According to Paul, they were in God, and God was in them.

Keen on koinōnia

Yes, it is true they had their differences of opinion, they had many difficulties to overcome, they had major problems that needed sorted out, they had their individual personalities but, in spite of these and, in spite of each other, they were one in Christ.

The depth of fellowship they experienced was not shallow or superficial. It was not a fuzzy feeling generated by a few minutes chat over a cup of tea and sticky bun, or a mug of coffee and donut, or coke and cookies. It was rich. It was real. It cemented their lives together. It was a practical down-to-earth support system. There was a splendid sense of unity in the Spirit. There was a cohesive bond that they dearly treasured.

D L Moody recognised this wonderful truth when he said: 'There are two ways of being united—frozen together and melted together!' In the church of Jesus Christ, we are not frozen together by formalism, rusted together by ritualism, linked together by liberalism, or chained together by conservatism—we are melted together by the maestro of the Holy Spirit.

They were in it together. Partners in *koinōnia*. And it was like that from day one for Paul speaks of their relationship from *the first (prōtos) day until now.* They have taken out shares in the mission of the gospel. Their brand of fellowship was an expression of vibrant, authentic Christianity in action. It is apparent from chapter one that:

- their *partnership* in the gospel (*cf.* verse 5),
- promoted the *advance* of the gospel (*cf.* verse 12), and
- it guarded the *faith* of the gospel (*cf.* verse 27).

Family album

Seems incredible ... but, remember, that is the way it was. Flick the pages and look at some of the foundation members. They were as different as chalk and cheese. On the face of it, there is nothing that would cause them to gel. It was all sorts of people, they were a mixed bag.

On a purely human level, we would not find them living on the same street, let alone find them worshipping in the same church—and enjoying it!

Lydia was there! She was a wealthy businesswoman from Thyatira who made her fortune selling purple cloth, a cloth that featured in the power dressing of the rich and influential of her day. She was obviously well-heeled and upper middle class and would have climbed the social ladder with comparative ease. Hers was a lifestyle of affluence. And yet she did not receive any special grade of life more suited to her bank balance.

The anonymous slave girl was there! This poor soul is a pathetic sight—demented, degraded, and demon-possessed. She lived her life in the gutter and sold her body so as to scrape together a meagre existence. For her, life was hardly worth living. And yet she did not receive an inferior quality of life just because she was a street woman from the slums.

The jailer was there! He was on the brink of committing suicide before Paul talked him out of it. He lived his life on a knife edge because of the heavy weight of responsibility resting on his shoulders and because of the uncertain whims of his employers. He was a decent sort of bloke earning a good wage. He comes across as a family man. And yet just because he was who he was, he did not get anything different in terms of the package offered to him at his conversion.

All one, not all the same

The eternal life given to all three converts was exactly the same. The saving grace experienced by each of them was precisely the same. The Lord they trusted was the same person. There is no difference. None at all.

That is what we need to remember—no matter who we are, no matter what we are, no matter where we are from—the life we have in Christ is the same for every member in God's global family. We are, in the eyes of God, on an equal footing. God does not make fish of one and flesh of another. Favouritism is not in the divine vocabulary. Thank God, he makes no difference. Why should we?

God is the great equaliser.

Can you imagine?

- Lydia standing at the kitchen sink washing the dishes after a fellowship meal! Why not?

- The slave girl standing at the front of the church leading the people in a time of praise and worship! Why not?
- The jailer standing in the vestibule greeting everyone who turns up for worship with a warm handshake or perhaps a holy kiss! Why not?

This is the essence—the pith—of new life in Christ. Discrimination in God's international family is neither politically correct nor spiritually sensitive. God is not into racism or bigotry. When it comes to grace, apartheid is a no-go area. As far as Paul is concerned, such a warped attitude is a total non-starter for God does not play favourites.

On my mind

When Paul reflects on his early days in Philippi, he is excited and jubilant, his heart is filled with gladness and his mind is uplifted. 'For the man who has forgotten to be thankful,' writes Robert Louis Stevenson, 'is the man who has fallen asleep in life.' I find it quite remarkable that, even when he is confined to barracks and going nowhere for the foreseeable future, Paul is constantly thinking of others, not himself. And every recollection he has brings incalculable joy and undiluted pleasure. Precious memories! For him, how they linger.

There was so much that happened to Paul in Philippi, the memory of which could produce considerable pain and sorrow. It seems that the Lord in his grace and tender mercy healed his damaged emotions and enabled him to cope with such times when life did not seem fair. Sometimes bad things do happen to good people.

Paul was illegally arrested and hauled before the court on a series of trumped-up charges. Both he and his companion Silas were 'severely flogged' before being 'thrown into prison' (Acts 16:23). Apparently they were a security risk so they were put in the 'inner cell' and fastened to the stocks (Acts 16:24). It was the ultimate in humiliation and horror.

Even those memories brought joy for it was through his suffering that the prison warder and his immediate family found Jesus as Lord and Saviour. God works in strange ways. (And that is not a reference to a prison in Manchester, UK.)

Paul learned to look on the bright side—the sunny side—because he knew God was in complete control of every situation. Paul learned to laugh at his troubles and he never ran out of things to laugh at. He was 'chained and cheerful' (George Mitchell) because he discovered the unbeatable value of viewing events on earth from the perspective of heaven and from the lofty vantage point of God's immovable throne. Things are different when we look at them through the lens of eternity (*cf.* Isaiah 6, Daniel 2, Revelation 4). In comparison with the numberless aeons of everlastingness, Paul's temporary trials fade into oblivion.

The story is told of eighty-year-old Mary Ann who, during a very strong Californian earthquake, remained serene and unafraid. Some questioned her sanity and whether, perhaps, she was in denial or in the late stages of senility. Others conjectured that perhaps she had been through an earthquake before and that a former survival experience had led to her calm and hopeful demeanour. Still others felt that maybe, at her age, she simply had no fear of dying.

Mary Ann, however, offered this explanation when a reporter asked her: 'Why weren't you afraid?'

'I never even thought about being afraid,' she said. 'I was too busy rejoicing at the truth that I serve a God who is able to shake the whole world!'

Echoes of Helen Keller. I think so. She once said: 'Resolve to keep happy, and your joy shall form an invincible host against difficulty.' Sounds like Paul.

A gut reaction

It is possible to have people on our minds without having them on our hearts. Paul not only thinks about them, he feels for them. So we read: *It is right (dikaios) for me to feel (phroneō) this way about all of you, since I have you in my heart (kardia).* In effect, Paul was saying: 'As I share with you my feelings, I open my whole inner being to you and tell you that the level of my affection is deep and tender.'

Paul was not curious.

There is a vast difference between sticking your nose in other people's business and putting your heart into their problems.

Paul cared. Deeply. Honestly. His sincere love for them could not be disguised or hidden. They were on his heart. That is a good place to carry people. If you carry them on your nerves, you will get a good case of the jitters. If you carry them on your neck, you are sure to get a dose of hypertension. If you carry them on your stomach, you will end up with an ulcer. They were on his heart. It was not dependent on his personal situation for his compassionate care was born out of a bona fide concern for them. Love is the tie that binds.

It is not just a select few that Paul feels this way about—an exclusive handful, as it were. No, it is *about all of you.* There are no exceptions. Not one! He does not have the clique mentality for his love embraces every single person in the assembly—the good, bad, and indifferent.

The big question: how does he do it? It was *the affection of Christ Jesus* channelled through Paul to them. Like Paul, when John Fawcett (1740-1817) reflected on the handful of people in the small Baptist Chapel in Yorkshire, England that God had entrusted to him, he penned the words:

Blest be the tie that binds
Our hearts in Christian love;
The fellowship of kindred minds
Is like to that above.

- Paul loved them for the sake of Jesus.
- Paul loved them because of Jesus.
- Paul loved them through Jesus.

The Greek word *splanchnon* means that Paul has a heart passion for them. The burden of them upon his heart is such that his heart aches and pines for them. That is love with a capital L. Front line love. It has been well said that:

- Love has eyes that see human needs.
- Love has ears that hear human needs.
- Love has feet that run to meet human needs.
- Love has hands that minister to human needs.

Souls and soles

Many years ago, on a bitterly cold day in February, a little boy was standing barefoot in front of a shoe store in New York. A woman riding up the street in a beautiful carriage saw him and ordered her driver to stop. She alighted from her carriage and quickly went to the boy. 'My little fellow, why are you looking so earnestly in that window?'

'I was asking God to give me a pair of shoes,' he replied, shivering. The woman took him by the hand and went into the store. She asked the proprietor for half-a-dozen pairs of socks. She also asked for a basin of warm water and a towel. When he brought them to her, she took the boy to the back of the store, removed her gloves, knelt down, washed his grimy feet, and dried them with the towel.

She then had him put on a pair of socks. Returning to the front of the store, she bought him a pair of shiny black shoes. As they parted she said: 'I hope, my little fellow, that you are more comfortable.'

He caught her hand and, with tears in his eyes, replied to her: 'Are you God's wife?' If we love God, it will show.

In my prayers

The proof that these good folks mean so much to Paul is seen in the fact that he prays for them and, when he does, it is *always (pantote) ... with joy (chara)*. A T Robertson defines Paul's joyful prayer life in this letter as 'a spiritual rhapsody'. The apostle has a prayer list and their names are near the top. They are often targeted at the throne of grace and that is what strengthened their bond of fellowship.

Every church Paul founded was an answer to prayer, every letter Paul wrote was born from a heart of prayer, every sermon Paul preached was bathed in the power of prayer. Paul prayed sensibly, specifically, sensitively, and supernaturally. There is power in prayer. Nuclear power.

How easy it is to pray for people who give us reason to be grateful. They often prove to be accepting and affirming, real instead of phoney, supportive and giving rather than subversive and grabby. It is so important that we pray for one another for talking to God about his people is no less rated than talking to his people about God.

My friend Ken Trivette of Chattanooga, Tennessee tells the story of a little child who travelled alone from Scotland down to London to have a series of operations for her twisted body. Because of the distance, she had to leave her family behind—such was life back then.

A sympathetic nurse took her under her wing, she showered her with care and affection. She tried her best to help the wee girl settle into the monotonous routine of hospital life fairly quickly. One day, after meeting so many people for the first time, the nurse asked her: 'Do you have any questions?' 'Yes,' she said, 'it's been great meeting all these people but who is going to pray for me?'

Prayer enabled Paul to cross the miles from where he was to where they were. I believe Paul is a sterling example of an intercessor, a man in the mould of Abraham and Moses—he was off his seat and on his knees making contact with God on their behalf. In that sense, Paul had the ear of God.

No unfinished symphony

Paul exudes confidence when he says: *being confident (peithō) of this, that he who began (enarchomai) a good work (ergon) in you will carry it on to completion (epiteleō) until the day (hēmera) of Christ Jesus.* Here is a relationship where the Lordship of Christ is of paramount importance, a fellowship where the Lord is central. God has an agenda and he is sticking to it. He will not be blown off-course for God never does anything by halves.

One of the insuperable joys of Christian ministry is the anticipation of what the church will ultimately become.

A look at the evangelical church today can be a little disheartening and discouraging, but a look at what the church will become in the future is fantastically exciting. This was Paul's focus, his honest conviction.

Bookends of life

The intention here is to show that God is actively at work. The Philippians' salvation is something which God initiated and which he continues to be involved in. One day he will bring it to a grand finale. Paul describes it beautifully when he says it is a *good* work. The Greek word *agathon* can also be translated 'noble'. So from start to finish, salvation is a noble work in the hearts and lives of ignoble people.

It is the same for us—the goal is our glorification—the magic moment when we will be like Jesus. When Christ gets involved in a person's life, he always finishes what he starts. He commences in order to continue— he continues in order to complete. The end product of a redeemed life is another person in the image of God. The finished work of the Lord Jesus is another sinner transformed into a replica of Christ himself.

That glorious day—already circled in the Father's diary—will herald a wonderful passing-out parade of all those to whom God has applied the finishing touches. We can look at it like this:

- I am not what I used to be, and
- I may not be what I ought to be, but
- I am not yet what I am going to be!

At home Lois and I have a message magnet attached to the fridge door. It reads: *Be patient! God's not finished with me yet!* True. God has not written me off, he has not ditched me, he has not sidelined me. He just keeps on working in my life. He chisels away at the rough edges of my faith and character. He takes the raw material at his disposal and shapes it into a life that is commendable to him.

The story is told of the sculptor whose statue of a horse fascinated and caught the admiration of everyone. One day he was asked: 'How did you take such an ugly, unpretentious piece of stone and make such a beautiful image of a horse?' His answer: 'I simply chipped away everything that didn't look like a horse!' That is what God is doing in our lives—he is still working on me to make me what I ought to be.

Michelangelo, it is said, was walking past a discarded piece of marble when he exclaimed: 'I see an angel in there!' His remarkable genius could see the awesome potential that others overlooked. Similarly, Jesus Christ comes along, he can see endless possibilities in us—he can see today what we can be tomorrow.

The story is told of a painter who saw a beggar whose clothes were tattered, his hair unkempt, and his face dirty. The artist decided to paint the man as he might have looked if he had the dignity of a job and a good home to go to. When he invited the beggar to see the painting, he did not recognise himself.

'That's me?' he asked.

'Yes,' said the artist, *'that's what I see in you.'*

For the first time in decades the aging man was given hope. He promised: *'By God's grace, I'm going to be the kind of man you see me to be!'*

One day a fairly cynical gentleman met a lady friend in the shopping mall. Over a cup of coffee, she related to him the story of her recent conversion to Jesus Christ. That prompted him to ask the question: 'What if somehow when it all ends and you die, you find yourself in hell, not in heaven—what then?' The relatively new convert looked him in the eye and said: 'If I lose my soul, God will lose more. I will only lose my soul but God will lose his honour!'

Take heart. God is on the ball. He has not kicked it into touch. When he does, the final whistle will have blown, the game will be over—and, believe it or not, we will be perfect. The future is bright. In fact, so bright that 'when I look into it,' says Oprah Winfrey, 'it burns my eyes!'

1:9

Marbles and grapes

Some time back I was given a copy of the most wonderful book, *No Greater Power*, penned by a former chaplain to the United States Senate. In it, Richard Halverson writes: 'Crush marbles and you get fragmentation, disintegration—hard, sharp pieces. You can get hurt if you're not careful. Crush grapes and you get fragrant, refreshing wine.

'Some people relate like marbles. The fear of vulnerability hardens them. They protect themselves, allow no one to penetrate. Being vulnerable is high risk, and they want low risk. They bump against others and ricochet around, never enjoying a vital relationship. In brittle lovelessness, they shatter when crushed, and hurt others.

'Some people relate like grapes. They yield to pressure. They accept their weakness as essential to intimacy. They give love, knowing love is vulnerable, knowing love is the heart and soul of our faith. When crushed, they bring blessing: fragrant, redemptive blessing.'

That was the experience of the Christians in Philippi. Like a cluster of grapes they were caught in the winepress of severe trial and affliction. Unlike those with the marble mindset, they yielded to God. Consequently, their lives exuded a wine full of faith and fragrant with love.

They were not sour in their attitude to the Lord. They were the epitome of sweetness. There was love manifested in their interpersonal relationships and a deep sense of commitment to each other in the local assembly. Paul says: 'Hey folks, that's good! Now, let's see if we can do better!' He wants them to push the boat out even further.

Only the best will do

Paul tells them the substance of his prayer: *that your love may abound more and more in knowledge and depth of insight.* Quite specific is Paul. This is quality love. Nothing but the best. It is not something hollow or superficial, neither is it a shallow form of sentimental emotionalism.

It is spiritual love, *agapē* love, divine love. This is the kind of virtue that is geared to the other person's highest good. It does not think: 'What can I get out of this?' On the contrary, it seeks to enhance the other person's life to such a degree that they will pause and give thanks to God for such a display of no strings attached love. This is John 3:16 love. Calvary love.

We hear Paul pray. Believing prayer. We feel his heart beat. We take his pulse. We sense the intensity of his longing as he passionately yearns for their maturity.

Two midgets, dressed to kill and sporting the latest fashion accessories, boarded a street car in downtown Vancouver. They were hardly forty inches high, but their faces revealed at least thirty years of real life struggle. As they found a seat, a hush of stunned amazement came over the other commuters.

A young man, sitting directly behind the little lady, was so overcome that he blurted out in a stage whisper to the person sitting beside him:

'Dwarfs!' That made the little lady see red! She quickly turned around and, with a look of indignation, snapped: 'Excuse me! Midgets, not dwarfs!'

You see, even a midget does not like to think that his life is dwarfed. Stunted growth is not a desirable commodity in the lives of God's people. There is no need for us to be spiritual pygmies. Paul wants them (and us) to grow—to grow in grace, and to grow up in Christ.

The Niagara syndrome

Paul desired a greater expression of their love. He was not content with what was present already. Wonderful as that may have been, he wanted more. He did not want them to rest on their hard-earned laurels and settle down in premature, middle class, cushioned comfort.

He longed for their love to *abound* like a river bursting its banks. The Greek word *perisseuō* has the idea of 'overflowing, wave upon wave, cascading like a waterfall'. What a phenomenal picture of love in action—not inaction—for this is the Niagara syndrome. This kind of love cannot be measured or contained, it overflows. It is lavish and generous. It keeps time with the beating heart of Jesus. It is a love that is unrestricted and unrestrained, we cannot keep it back, but we can direct its course.

Paul is extremely careful in his choice of words. When he used the word *abound* he was referring to the extent of their love in that it should be reaching out to more and more people. When he added the words *more and more (mallon)* he was drawing attention to the effectiveness of their ministry outreach. He wanted them to learn how to love more people and love them all better. It is a matter of improving the quality of our service. How we do it is important.

I heard about a man who used to drive all the way across town to get to church on a Sunday morning. It took him twenty minutes to get there and, en route, he passed by many places of worship. One day the senior deacon popped the question: 'Tell me, George, why do you pass all these other churches in order to come to our church?' George thought for a moment and then he said: 'Because they love a fellow here!'

Abounding love cannot be bound. It is not confined to those we like, or those who like us, or even those we would like to have like us. It is not selective. It does not require an assurance that it will be reciprocated.

Yes, we can love the lovely, the lovable, and the loving—but this brand of love embraces all men. All shapes, all sizes, all sorts. This love is wide enough to love the unloved and the unlovely—it has a rescue mission mentality.

'Heat makes all things expand. And the warmth of love will always expand a person's heart.' (Chrysostom)

1:10

20/20 vision

The love we are thinking about here blossoms best when it is regulated. Paul talks about *knowledge (epignōsis) and depth (pas) of insight (aisthēsis)*. That suggests it not only involves the heart but the mind as well. When the heart and mind are in harmony, we have discerning love and loving discernment.

Paul Rees expressed it well when he wrote that '... light without love can be as forbiddingly cold as an iceberg in moonlight whilst love without light can be as flamingly destructive as a forest fire in the dry season.'

Love grows best in the soil of knowledge. It is not a matter of letting our hearts rule our heads. We not only need sentiment, we need sense. Our love will be controlled by the word of God and dictated by the parameters of Scripture. The love that we exercise toward others will be synchronised with the unclouded teaching of the Lord Jesus. This is a love that knows. An informed love. An intelligent love.

Contrary to the romanticist, Saint Valentine's Day view, real love is not blind. Genuine love will not deaden our critical faculties—it will have 20/20 vision. Not dimmed. Not blurred. It is perceptive, cataract free, and will meet the needs of others by conforming to the truth. It is not a sudden adrenaline rush. I agree with Philip Greenslade when he writes that 'we do not do our theology or worship only with our hormones.'

Spiritual radar

Paul goes a step further down the road when he says: *so that you may be able to discern (dokimazō) what is best (diapherō)*. Most of us would have little difficulty deciphering what is the difference between good and bad, but when we narrow it down to a higher level of better and best, it is not quite so easy.

On his eightieth birthday, someone asked Herbert Welch the secret of his serene spirit. He responded by saying: 'As I grow older, life becomes simpler, because I see the essentials more clearly in the evening light.'

The Greek word that Paul uses here for *insight* is the one from which we derive the word 'aesthetics', that is, our appreciation of what is beautiful and good. G H Morrison once said that you could tell a person who loves books or flowers by the way they handle them. So, he said, you can tell a person who loves people by the way she handles them. In that unique sense, love is a connoisseur in the fine art of appreciating and valuing people.

Our primary goal here is excellence. This love based on real knowledge and keen insight will enable us to accurately assess and evaluate every situation that presents itself to us—a type of spiritual radar that results in us making right and proper decisions.

The hymn writer, Edwin Hatch (1835-89), grasped the idea perfectly when he wrote:

That I may love what thou dost love,
And do what thou wouldst do.

When John Wesley went away to Oxford, his godly mother Susanna wisely wrote in one of her many letters to him: 'Whatever weakens your reason, impairs the tenderness of your conscience, obscures your sense of God, or takes off the delight for spiritual things, whatever increases the authority of your body over your mind, that thing is sin.'

Approval will only be given to that which is glorifying to the Lord. This will free us up to focus our time and energy on what really counts instead of being hijacked into a game of trivial pursuits. At the end of the day, it is all about priority living for this is not a 'one size fits all' love—it will tell us what is worth dying for and it will guide us in what is worth living for.

'I've learned that we must hold everything loosely, because when I grip it tightly, it hurts when my Father prises my fingers loose and takes it from me.' (Corrie ten Boom)

Glasshouse Christians

Paul's aspiration for the Philippian believers is that they *may be pure and blameless until the day of Christ.* There are two sides to this coin—the first speaks of purity. Personal integrity. Paul pulls no punches when he says the emphasis here is on the genuineness of the people who are involved in this expanding program of love. You can tell a lot about a man by the way he treats those who can do nothing for him.

The word *pure (eilikrinēs)* means we should be whiter than white. Our lives should be above and beyond reproach. There should be an openness and transparency about us. We may not opt to live in a proverbial glasshouse but Joe Public should be able to see right through us—nothing to hide, no skeletons hanging in the closet. Charles Spurgeon said that 'character needs no epitaph—you can bury a man but his character will beat the hearse back from the graveyard!'

If we live like that, sincerity will be the hallmark of our lives. In other words, when our lives are exposed to the bright rays of sunlight, there should be no telltale cracks of hypocrisy. That means we will be on the inside what we appear to be on the outside. There will be a ring of reality to all that we profess for a man's best collateral is his character. Our actions will not be a contradiction of our words.

John MacArthur reminds us: 'Living the life of integrity is like baking bread. It is not enough merely to pour all the right ingredients together in a pan, stick it in the oven, and hope to produce bread. All the ingredients must first be properly mixed so that every ingredient touches every other ingredient to form a common, cohesive, single whole.' That means the Christian life is one that fits together and works together—we are what we are because we are who we are.

The poet, Harry Hein, put it like this:

Be who you is,
Because if you is who you ain't,
You ain't who you is!

Well, that sonnet may have a minimum of eloquence, but it maximises common sense. And it is powerfully true. I believe we should be living our lives in such a way that we would not mind giving the family parrot to the town gossip.

Stepping stones

The word *blameless (aproskopos)* refers to relational integrity. It means living a life that does not cause others to stumble. In all my dealings in love with other people and groups, I should seek to be a stepping stone, rather than a stumbling block. We should not be like an uneven footpath (sidewalk) against which a man could stub his toe and fall.

If a person is an offence, he does that which causes another to fall into one of Satan's traps. Paul's desire was that these believers would live so that no one would ever stumble because of their behaviour.

The apostle reminds them of the approaching *day (hēmera) of Christ* as an incentive to be known as men and women of integrity. This is a reference to the day when believers will stand before the judgment seat of Christ for the purpose of assessment (*cf.* 2 Corinthians 5:10). It is the day when our lives will come under the searching scrutiny of our blessed Lord. This is the moment when, after a personal interview with Jesus, rewards will be handed out to those who have been loyal and faithful to him.

We are responsible down here and we are accountable over there.

1:11

Productivity pays

Paul concludes his prayer on a high note when he writes of them being *filled with the fruit (karpos) of righteousness (dikaiosynē) that comes through Jesus Christ—to the glory (doxa) and praise (epainos) of God.* He is not principally interested in a busy flurry of hurly-burly activity but in the kind of spiritual fruit that is yielded when we are in fellowship with the living Christ.

It is God who produces this kind of fruit in the life of the Christian—however, the secret is our abiding in Christ (*cf.* John 15:1-8). When we do, we will bear fruit (*cf.* John 15:2), more fruit (*cf.* John 15:2), much fruit (*cf.* John 15:5), and much more fruit (*cf.* John 15:8). Our lives will be richly productive.

What is the fruit he longs to see reproduced in us? There is the 'fruit of the Spirit' (Galatians 5:22, 23) which is a balanced, healthy life that resonates to the praise of God. Paul compares winning people to Jesus Christ as bearing fruit (*cf.* Romans 1:13, 15:28). We are exhorted to 'bear fruit in every good work' (Colossians 1:10) and 'to offer to God a sacrifice of praise—the fruit of lips that confess his name' (Hebrews 13:15).

Fruit, therefore, comes in all shapes and sizes. When our faith works and our love abounds, a ripened harvest is inevitable. And God is glorified. At that stage, Paul's prayer will be answered in their lives. Similarly, will it be answered in your life and mine?

God is looking for spiritual fruit, not religious nuts.

French connection

When Lawrence of Arabia was in Paris after World War 1, he took some of his friends to show them a few of the splendid sights of the city: the Louvre, the Arc de Triomphe, Napoleon's Tomb at Les Invalides, and the Champs Elysées. Amazingly, they found little interest in these touristy places.

The thing that really gripped their imagination was the faucet in the bathtub of their hotel room. They spent a lot of time there turning it on and off—they thought it was wonderful. All they had to do was turn the handle and they could get all the water they wanted.

Sometime later, when they were ready to leave Paris and return to the East, Lawrence found them in the bathroom trying to detach the faucet. 'You see,' they said, 'it is very dry in Arabia. What we need are faucets. If we have them, we will have all the water we want.'

Lawrence had to explain that the effectiveness of the faucets did not lie in themselves but in the immense system of water works to which they were attached. He had to point out that behind this lay the rain and snowfall on the Alps.

Many of God's people today are living lives that are as dry and dusty as the deserts of Arabia. They have the faucets, but there is no connection to the pipeline. That is the difference God makes when our lives are intimately and relationally linked to his—there is refreshment and spiritual fruit. All we need do is turn on the tap.

1:12

A handle on happenings

I reckon the veteran Paul deserves a medal. Why? What is so special about him? Let him speak for himself, this is what he says: *Now I want you to know (ginōskō), brothers (adelphos), that what has happened (kata) to me has really served (erchomai) to advance (prokopē) the gospel.* Superb.

Paul knows how to handle himself in the good times as well as the bad times. When everything seemed to be falling apart, he sensed that God was still in control. When all he had was a handful of shattered dreams and popcorn ambitions, he still believed that the sovereign God would make Romans 8:28 a living reality. Someone said if we see Jesus in our circumstances then we will see our circumstances in Jesus.

Life for the apostle had taken a dramatic downturn. Even to a seasoned optimist, it would still appear as though Paul was destined for a rough, hair-raisingly bumpy ride on the rollercoaster of life. Alas, he is finding out quickly—very quickly—that life is no joyride in an amusement arcade or themed pleasure park. Life has its high walled prisons as well as its palaces. Paul's life seems to be collapsing around him like a deck of cards. For him, this was an abrasive rub with reality.

Best of times, worst of times

When we take the lid off the phrase, *what has happened to me*, it appears as though the dominoes are falling all around him. Yet, because of his wonderfully upbeat attitude, Paul smiles through suffering. His outlook shows us how we can make the best of times out of our worst of times.

The nagging pain is taken out of his adversity because he trusts God implicitly. His understanding of Providence was not airy-fairy or even mystically pie-in-the-sky, it was earthed in personal experience. Even though the tapestry of life seems to be no more than a series of twisted knots, Paul does not start questioning: 'Why? Why this? Why me? Why now?'

Paul knew what he was talking about. He did not believe in putting a question mark where God put a period. And, be assured, it was not out of the top of his head. This was life. Real life. Life in the raw.

It is not unlike the stirring testimony of Betsie ten Boom as she lay dying in the Ravensbrück Concentration Camp. When nearing the end of her life, she uttered a sentence which has travelled around the world. *'There is,'* she said, *'no pit so deep that Christ is not deeper still.'* Bruised and assaulted by a Nazi rifle, humiliated by the Holocaust, she said to her sister Corrie: *'They will listen to us because we've been there!'*

A political football

Paul desperately wanted to go to Rome. It was number one on his list of 'places I must visit'. Not just to see the sights and buy the tourist memorabilia but to tell Nero and his fellow citizens of his encounter with the living Lord. In that day, Rome was comparable to the Oval Office or Number 10 Downing Street—the place of ultimate clout and decision making. Paul 'wanted to go to Rome as a preacher, instead he went as a prisoner' (Warren Wiersbe).

Actually, it all began to go drastically wrong when he arrived in the golden city of Jerusalem. The preacher man was illegally arrested, falsely accused, and nearly lynched by a religious mob of fanatical extremists baying for his blood. They thought the only good preacher was a dead one.

In a classic case of mistaken identity, they told him he was someone that he was not—an Egyptian renegade high on their wanted list (*cf.* Acts 21:38). Paul became a political football kicked all over the place. He was moved from pillar to post. He was like a fly enmeshed in the tangled web of politics.

There was one court appearance after another. And then, to add insult to injury, he was given a complimentary, one way ticket for a Mediterranean cruise. On top of that, there was a hurricane that caused the ship to run aground off the island of Malta. Three months and a few days later he reached Rome where he was imprisoned. For the best part of two years he was virtually forgotten as he waited for the outcome of his appeal. The odds seemed unbeatable.

In light of this, one of the most challenging assignments we all face is to interpret the tragedies of life in such a way that they become bearable.

If only ..! If only we could read God's diary! If only we could understand his hidden purposes!

Putting on a brave face

I think it would be natural for Paul to react in an aggressive manner to all the mishaps in his life. It just seemed as though everything was going wrong. He could have kicked the garden fence or gone down to the gym and vented his spleen on a leather punch bag. Or he could have put the blame fairly and squarely on other people. In so doing he would have left himself wide open for blackmail from the adversary himself. He would only be hammering a few nails in his own coffin as the root of bitterness would surely entwine itself around his heart.

Or he could have wallowed in the Slough of Despond and become depressed and immobile. Like quicksand, he would be sucked under by his circumstances. I imagine another knee-jerk reaction would be for him to postpone his feelings by adopting the Scarlett O'Hara syndrome: 'I'll think about it tomorrow!' He could let them simmer by placing them on the back burner over a low blue flame—on the surface all seems calm, but underneath his feelings seethe.

Thankfully, Paul did not react in any one of those ways. He had an alternative. Says Paul: 'OK, it's bad, but it's not the end of the world! It could have been worse! Much worse!'

Keeping your head above water

Paul realised that God had an agenda for his life. From this most harrowing experience, he instinctively says in a voice etched with sincere conviction:

it has really served to advance the gospel. Fantastic spirit, man. That is the way to look at it. Never say die. Suppressing this man is like trying to sink a cork in a bath. He is irrepressible. Indomitable.

We do not find Paul licking his wounds in a corner. He is not sulking because he is, quite literally, confined to barracks. He is not feeling sorry for himself at all. He does not even feel inconvenienced. He certainly does not give me the impression of a man coming apart at the seams because of the intolerance of an oppressive regime. Far from it.

He reminds me of that saintly Scotsman from Anwoth by the Solway Firth, Rev Samuel Rutherford (1600-61). In 1637, like the apostle, imprisoned for his faith, he wrote from his prison cell in the granite city of Aberdeen: 'Christ triumphs in me. This is my palace not my prison. I think this is all, to gain Christ. All other things are shadows, dreams, fancies, and nothing.'

1:13

Opportunity knocks

The apostle is buoyant in his faith, relishing the opportunities that God in his unique way has brought to him. He does not have to go looking for a congregation, they come to him. That is why we read: *As a result (hostē), it has become clear (phaneros) throughout the whole palace guard (praitōrion) and to everyone else that I am in chains for Christ.*

Twenty-four hours a day, seven days a week, Paul was shackled with an eighteen-inch chain to a Roman soldier. The roster was such that every six hours the shift changed. So Paul had four potential prospects for salvation every day of the week. During his two year internment, he would have had no fewer than three thousand witnessing opportunities. Terrific.

Paul may have been locked up but he was not tongue-tied when it came to sharing his faith in Jesus. Paul was in his element, he had a captive audience. The guards had no option but to listen—they could not help but hear what he said. And the outcome was such that some of these crack, hand-picked, double-pay, imperial troops were gloriously converted.

Paul, technically, may have been a prisoner of Rome, but that is not the way he viewed his incarceration. He believed he was *in chains for*

Christ. The amazing thing is that other people see it that way as well for it has become widely known in the community.

The six million dollar question: how did it become known? Let us face it, there were thousands of prisoners and one chained man looks much the same as another. As J A Motyer says: 'The manacles tell nothing, but the man does!' It did not matter who visited Paul or whether he was all alone with his military escort, the conversation and chitchat were always the same—it was all Christ.

That reminds me of a story I heard about the cello player who kept his finger on the one spot. After one performance, he was approached by a member of the audience who asked him: 'Sir, why don't you move your hand up and down like the other people?' The musician—he had to be Irish—replied: 'Ma'am, they're looking for it, I've found it!'

Paving the way

The gospel triumphed. It was unstoppable. It made significant inroads into the heart of Rome itself. Phenomenal. The Greek term Paul used is most colourful. For example, it was used in ancient times to describe a group of pioneer woodcutters who preceded an advancing army, clearing the way through an otherwise impenetrable forest of trees and underbrush. It is a military term that was used by engineers who prepared a road for a battalion of troops by removing all obstructions.

Thus Paul viewed his circumstances as having cleared the way for the gospel to progress into the nerve centre of the vast Roman empire. This was no setback.

It was a small step for Paul but it was a giant leap forward for the gospel of Jesus Christ.

1:14

The ripple effect

In the cold light of day, Paul reflects and says: *Because of my chains, most of the brothers in the Lord have been encouraged (peithō) to speak (laleō) the word (logos) of God more courageously (tolmaō) and fearlessly (aphobōs).* It seems to me that others are influenced by our lives more than we realise sometimes. This was the impetus some of them needed to engage in the cut and thrust of personal evangelism and soul winning. It added a sparkling new dimension to their varied ministry. There was a definite boldness to their witnessing that was not there before. It gave a sharp cutting edge to their proclamation of the gospel message.

The hymnwriter, William Cowper (1731-1800), draws the threads together with the conclusion that *God moves in a mysterious way, his wonders to perform.* So far as I am concerned, what does it matter so long as God moves?

The story is told of two friends who were talking together, one older and wiser, the other younger and passing through a severe trial. The older friend, with loving wisdom, said: 'No moment will ever again be like this; let there be something for Jesus in it!' That bullish mindset is what kept Paul going—in his imprisonment, he wanted there to be 'something for Jesus' in it.

'The same God who used Moses' rod, Gideon's pitchers, and David's sling, used Paul's chains.' (Warren Wiersbe)

1:15-18

Tackling professional jealousy

Paul is not looking for the sympathy vote because of the restrictions he is facing nor is he so insular that he cannot be rational about what is happening in the outside world. It is clear that Paul is not looking through Pollyannaish spectacles for he knows there are a handful of folks who are tenaciously determined to do him harm. He is no fool. By the same token, as a counterbalance, there are others who are fiercely loyal in their unswerving support of him.

Some of these guys want to pour high octane fuel on the fiery trial Paul is experiencing because they do not really care about him as a person. For them it is *carpe diem*—they seize the moment and take advantage of the situation and *stir up (egeirō) trouble (thlipsis) for [him] while [he is] in chains.*

For reasons best known to himself, Paul chose not to dwell on what they did to him. To be honest, we do not know exactly what it was and it is a fruitless exercise for us to engage in speculation. Whatever it was, they did him no favours. Paul was not desensitised as a person, he had his feelings just as much as the next man and he must have been hurt by their actions. Their below the belt, unsporting punches would have left him winded. They were adding insult to injury as they ladled salt upon his wounds.

Stuart Briscoe describes Paul like this: 'Whatever we may think of Paul, he had a temper that got heated and feelings that got hurt. He was no computerised theological machine churning out inspired writings, but a very warm human individual who needed as much love as the next man, and then some. You cannot hurt a computer's feelings or grieve a theological concept, but you can destroy a man. Paul was destructible, but he was not destroyed. And it was not for lack of somebody trying!

'The perspective that he had discovered allowed him to say that he did not really mind what happened to him so long as nothing happened to stop the gospel because, in his understanding, the message preached mattered more than the man preaching.'

Partisan preachers

It was not so much who was doing it, it was the way they were going about it. That was what really bothered him. Some of them were preaching Christ *out of envy (phthonos) and rivalry (eris)*. As Paul described those who were preaching for the wrong reasons, he used an interesting Greek word, *eritheia*. He said they were preaching *out of selfish ambition*. It has the idea of 'canvassing for office in order to get people to support you'. It was party politics.

They were jockeying for positions of influence within the local Christian community. They were wheeler-dealing in all kinds of behind-closed-doors, clandestine manoeuvres. As we say, they were up to no good. Their aim was to get people to follow them—Paul's goal was to get people to follow Jesus Christ. What a difference.

Big deal

Paul plainly asks the question: *But what does it matter?* There is no way that Paul was going to get dragged into throwing mud at people, especially those who professed faith in his Lord and Saviour. It deeply concerned him but he did not lose any sleep over it. It was not worth it and, quite frankly, neither were they.

The apostle to the Gentiles had other ways of expending his energy instead of wasting time in a war of words with them. Arguing with them would achieve little or nothing—there was no point in Paul banging his head against a brick wall. He would end up with a sore head, not them!

Paul was walking a tightrope and he only maintained his sense of balance and perspective by keeping his two eyes focused and glued on the Lord. To put it mildly, these folks were a minor distraction as well as a pain in the neck. A slight irritation, I suppose. The kind of thing he could have done without.

All that mattered to Paul, however, was that *whether from false motives (prophasis) or true (alētheia), Christ is preached (katangellō).* And he was. Paul was happy with that even though he did not approve of, or endorse, their motives. This guy is amazing, he has a big heart and a broad pair of shoulders. He would take it on the chin even though it was designed to knock him out of action.

That explains the tongue-in-cheek comment: *And because of this I rejoice (chairō). Yes, and I will continue to rejoice.* In other words, under no circumstances was he going to permit them to get him down. The message is bigger than the man. Always. God may bypass the man but he will always bless the message of Christ and him crucified.

As the nineteenth-century Scottish minister John Eadie wisely commented: 'The virtue lies in the gospel, not in the gospeller; in the exposition, not in the expounder.'

1:19

Holding the ropes

There is a story about a monastery in Portugal perched high on a 300-foot cliff. It can be reached only by a terrifying ride in a swaying basket. The basket is pulled with a single rope by several strong men who labour as they pull their cargo up the sheer cliff. One tourist became nervous as he began the journey because he noticed that the rope was old and frayed. 'How often do you change the rope?' he shouted to the monk as the trip

up the mountain began. 'Whenever it breaks!' came the reply.
Spine chilling. It does not bear thinking about, does it? The small print on the travel insurance policy would hardly encourage such a journey. Nevertheless, assuming the rope is in good condition, there should be no problem. The onus is on those who are holding the ropes. And this is what Paul draws attention to when he says with candid comment: *for I know that through your prayers (deēsis) and the help (epichorēgia) given by the Spirit (Pneuma) of Jesus Christ, what has happened to me will turn out (eis) for my deliverance (sōtēria).*

Every cloud has a silver lining

Paul sees his ultimate deliverance as dependent on two factors. There is the human input into his situation and there is the divine touch upon his life. Through their prayers they are holding the ropes. He valued enormously and treasured their prayerful interest and support. It meant so much to him to have the assurance that they were upholding him before the throne of grace.

O yes, he had prayed for them, now it was his turn to be on the receiving end. The ball was now back in his court. And he was elated and humbled— both at the same time. What he practised in his own life, he also profited from as it was lived out in others.

That is what kept him going, it made a mega difference to his outlook. It was the silver lining to the dark grey cloud of his confinement. Because he was the focus of their prayers, he was able to survive this particular crisis. Many of us have discovered that prayer can make all the difference between us hanging in there or calling it quits.

God is no man's debtor

Not only was Paul sustained by the prayers of the saints, he was also encouraged by the provision of the Spirit. The language that Paul used in this context is picturesque, the phrase literally means: 'the full supply of the Holy Spirit'. The word 'supply' or *help* is a double compound word which means 'to furnish supplies for a musical chorus'. In ancient times a benefactor would pay for the singers and the dancers at a festival (a kind of first-century sponsorship). In time, the word came to mean 'to provide generously'.

All the resources that heaven could muster were made freely available to Paul. There was no lack in God's supply, it just kept on flowing his way. It was lavish. And generous. It was just what he needed, and more. It seems to me that the thickest cloud often brings the heaviest shower of blessing.

Paul is quietly confident because he knows that God will continue to order events in his life. He is the divine choreographer so Paul places himself at his disposal. All these are links in the chain that will ultimately bring about his deliverance, in God's good time. And, remember, God is never late, he is never early, and he is never in a hurry—he is always on time.

For Paul, it is one day at a time. That is enough for any man to think about. He knew he would emerge from his ordeal with their prayers and the help of the Lord. He knew what he was experiencing was not the end, it would all turn out exactly as the sovereign God directed.

Things are not always as they seem!

Walter A. Maier told the story in *Decision* magazine of a shipwrecked man who was washed ashore on an uninhabited island. In the days that followed he painstakingly constructed a hut with a few things he salvaged from the wreck and from whatever he could find on the island. That little hut was the only protection he had from the harsh elements and the only place he could safeguard his possessions.

Upon returning one evening from a lengthy search for food, he was petrified to find the hut engulfed in flames. The loss devastated him. He was gutted. Needless to say, he spent that night despondent, sleeping on the sand.

He awoke early the next morning and, to his utter surprise, saw a ship anchored off the island. A crew member stepped ashore and told him: 'We saw your smoke signal and came to rescue you!'

On the face of it, what seemed like destruction turned out to be deliverance. The same principle held true for Paul in the city of Rome— God worked it all out. Paul needed to learn a lesson that we all need to grasp:

---

when all seems lost, it isn't!

1:20

Thinking today about tomorrow

Even though his back is to the wall, Paul continues to focus on the future. He is forward-looking and avidly planning ahead as he anticipates the day of his release. He writes: *I eagerly expect and hope (elpis)*. What a fantastic comment to make, it is one of itching expectation.

The Greek word *apokaradokia* actually has three elements wrapped up in its meaning. It is comprised of the words 'away', 'the head', and 'to watch'. When we put them all together, they convey the idea of watching something so intently that your head is turned away from everything else— it is the giraffe mindset for it refers to stretching the neck.

It is the single-mind syndrome—the *this one thing I do* philosophy favoured by Paul and his erstwhile contemporaries. It is all about setting a goal and going for it. His vision is not blurred, his sense of destiny has not diminished. He knows where he is going. And, given God's perfect time, he will get there. Typical Paul.

His hope is such that he is sitting on the edge of his seat. He is standing on his toes because his confidence has rocketed. It is sky-high. This spurs him on in his quest to be the kind of person God wants him to be. He does not want to have any regrets about his life, hence the phrase: *that I will in no way be ashamed (aischynomai)*. Paul wants to have an unblemished and untarnished testimony. Even though the pressure he is experiencing is enough to cause a mental blowout, he just wants to please the Lord in all his ways.

Plan B

The temptation for Paul is to make life easier for himself. Life would be an awful lot simpler if he clammed up and said nothing about his faith. The sound of silence in the short term would be golden. Instead, he prays that he *will have sufficient (pas) courage (parrēsia) so that now as always* he will be able to talk about the Lord with boldness.

Paul did not go softly, softly—if anything, he turned the volume up louder.

His supreme desire is reflected in the words that flow graciously from his quill on to the parchment. He longs that *Christ will be exalted (megalynō) in [his] body (sōma), whether by life (zōē) or by death (thanatos).* This was the driving force in Paul's life on planet earth. This was first-class dedication to a first-class cause. The objective for which he lived became the object on which he looked. That phrase has been freely translated to read: 'my body shall be the theatre in which the glory of Christ shall be exhibited.'

The logo of one missionary organisation is a picture of an ox with a plough on one side and an altar on the other. Underneath are the words: Ready for Either! That was Paul's motto for he knew the scales could swing either way.

Paul's immediate task, whatever the future turned out to be, is not to carry a digital image of Jesus Christ in his wallet (billfold) for occasional sharing with a few chosen people, but to show an enlarged, life-size Christ to all who care to look, a Christ displayed in Paul's every dimension and capacity—a Christ magnified in his body.

In their last letter home, prior to their martyrdom in China in December 1934, missionaries John and Betty Stam included this touching sentence: 'God knows what our end is, but we have decided that, by life or death, Christ shall be magnified.'

Like them, it did not matter where Paul was—in a prison or a pulpit, in a cell or a church, anywhere and everywhere—he just wanted his Lord and Saviour to be glorified in his body. If that meant life, great! If it spelt death, so what? From Paul's point of view, Jesus Christ is unrivalled. Peerless.

1:21

Paul's mission statement

What starts the adrenaline surging through Paul's veins? What turns him on? Here is the answer: *For to me, to live (zaō) is Christ and to die (apothnēskō) is gain (kerdos).* Jesus Christ was number one in his life. This was the motivational factor in all his ministry, the propelling thrust in all he sought to do. No wonder his life had such power, momentum, direction, and blessing. Charles Swindoll says that 'Paul forced every experience of life through the grid of his personal purpose statement.'

On one occasion William Booth, founder of the Salvation Army, was called to appear before Queen Victoria. Amidst her regal surroundings, she enquired: 'General Booth, what is the secret of your ministry? How is that others are so powerless and you are so mighty?' Booth looked into the face of the monarch and, with tears streaming down his cheeks, replied: 'Your Majesty, I guess the reason is because God has all there is of me.'

Here is the secret to living well and dying well. It comes down to the dynamics of our relationship with Jesus Christ. In the final analysis, when all is done and dusted, it is all about the centrality of Christ in the life of the individual. F B Meyer was on the right track when he wrote that 'Christ is the essence of our life, the model of our life, the aim of our life, the solace of our life, and the reward of our life.'

I will take the liberty and reword the verse—see if it makes sense to you. This is the acid test of our consecration to Christ:

- For me to live is *money*—to die is to leave it all behind.
- For me to live is *fame*—to die is to be quickly forgotten.
- For me to live is *power*—to die is to lose it all.
- For me to live is *things*—to die is to go empty-handed.

All of these fall flat. They fly in the face of contentment and happiness. They do not bring lasting joy. After a wild life of pleasure, Augustine (354-430), Bishop of Hippo in North Africa, confessed: 'O God, thou hast made us for thyself and our souls are restless until they find their rest in thee.'

When he was thirty-six, Lord Byron, the pampered darling of English high society, wrote in a poem:

My days are in the yellow leaf;
The flowers and fruits of love are gone;
The worm, the canker, and the grief
Are mine alone.

On a similar note, Robert Burns wrote in *Tam O'Shanter*:

Pleasures are like poppies spread,
You seize the flower, its blossom shed;
Or like the snow falls in the river,
A moment white—then melts for ever.

Only Christ can satisfy. Really satisfy. Unquestionably satisfy. That holds true, whether we do have or do not have, whether we are known or unknown, whether we live or die.

1:22-24

To go or not to go

If the *Peanuts* cartoons are to be believed, Charlie Brown has more than his fair share of frustrations. Like the one where Lucy is philosophising and Charlie is listening. As usual, Lucy has the floor, delivering one of her dogmatic lectures.

'*Charlie Brown,*' she begins, '*life is a lot like a deck chair. Some place it so they can see where they're going. Others place it to see where they've been. And some so they can see where they are at present.*'

Charlie sighs: '*I can't even get mine unfolded!*'

Talking about life and death, Paul has a similar problem. After a while it all becomes a little complicated. He is sitting on the horns of a dilemma and, for obvious reasons, that is not the most comfortable position to find yourself in! According to Ivor H. Evans in *Brewer's Dictionary of Phrase and Fable* this comes from the word 'lemma' which means something which is taken for granted, and a double 'lemma' is called a dilemma.

The picture conjured up by this phrase is that of someone facing a mad bull which is charging towards him and finding that if he tries to seize hold of one horn, the bull will simply toss him with the other. Basically, a no-win situation.

The normally decisive Paul cannot make up his mind—he does not know what to do—to do what is best for himself or to do what is more beneficial for them. He is caught between his keen desire to be with Christ personally and his overwhelming sense of duty to help the young and growing church at Philippi. He is between a rock and a hard place or, as he expressed it, he is *torn (synechō) between the two.*

It seems to me this guy is in a real quandary as he faces a titanic struggle. It is not a matter of drawing the shortest straw or making a decision based on the toss of a coin. It is not as easy as that. It rarely is.

I read the story of an older person who was standing on the deck of a cruise liner during a terrible storm. A concerned crew member approached her and advised her: 'Ma'am, you need to get inside pretty fast. It's dangerous to be out here, you could be swept overboard.' The woman deeply appreciated his comment but replied: 'I've got a daughter in New York and one in heaven and it doesn't matter to me which one I see next!'

A balancing act

We see Paul's line of reasoning when he writes: *If I am to go on living in the body, this will mean fruitful (karpos) labour (ergon) for me. Yet what shall I choose (haireomai)? I do not know (gnōrizō)! I am torn between the two: I desire (epithymia) to depart (analyō) and be with Christ, which is better (kreittōn) by far (polys); but it is more necessary (anankaios) for you that I remain (epimenō) in the body.* A tough one. Indeed.

Adoniram Judson (1788-1850) was the first overseas missionary sent out from America. In the early nineteenth century, he and his first wife went to Calcutta, India and, a short while later to Rangoon, Burma where he laboured for nearly four decades. After fourteen years he had a handful of converts and had managed to write a Burmese grammar.

During that time he suffered a horrible imprisonment for a year and a half and lost his wife and children to disease. Like Paul, he longed to be with the Lord, but also like the apostle, he considered his work for Christ to be infinitely more important than his personal comforts and longings. He therefore prayed that God would allow him to live long enough to translate the entire Bible into Burmese and to establish a church there of at least one hundred believers.

The Lord graciously granted that request and, as a bonus, he also allowed him to compile Burmese-English and English-Burmese dictionaries which became an invaluable resource to the Christian workers who followed in his footsteps. Judson wrote: 'If I had not felt certain that every trial was ordered by infinite love and mercy, I could not have survived my accumulated sufferings.'

'Paul is willing to postpone going to heaven in order to help Christians grow, and he is willing to go to hell in order to win the lost to Christ (*cf.* Romans 9:1-3).' (Warren Wiersbe)

The 'C' word

Commitment is the name of the game. Paul was committed to a cause and totally committed to Christ. When we look at what Paul is saying we quickly realise that it is not all cut and dried, there are pros and cons either way. Whatever decision is made, there would be huge advantages and big disadvantages. At the end of the day, he would be cast upon the Lord to lead and guide him in the path of his choosing.

How does Paul talk about death? In a fascinating way, he depicts it as 'a departure'. That is a most instructive word. It was used by soldiers when they took down their tents and moved on to another place.

Sailors were also familiar with this expression. To them it meant to loosen a ship from her moorings and set sail. When a ship would go out of the harbour, people would stand around watching as the ship sailed over the horizon. The term they frequently use is: 'there she goes'. But somewhere there is another harbour and, as that ship appears on the horizon, they say: 'here she comes'. For the Christian, that is a beautiful picture of death—it is a going out and a coming home.

It was also a term employed by the judiciary for it captured the moment when a prisoner would be released and set free. The farming community invoked the saying frequently for it signified the unyoking of a pair of oxen thereby removing their burden.

Death, therefore, held no ghastly terrors for Paul. He had nothing to fear or dread. For him it was no more than a change of location because the Lord was with him in either situation. To Paul, death did not put him six-foot under in a cemetery, it ushered him straight into the sanctuary.

German pastor Dietrich Bonhoeffer (1906-45) was of the same opinion when he said prior to being killed by the Nazis: *'This is the end; for me the beginning of life.'*

He was on the winning side whatever decision was made. That is what made the gargantuan question Paul wrestled with so unbelievably difficult to answer.

If he stayed ...

... the church at Philippi would reap a handsome dividend, they would benefit from the rich biblical ministry of Paul and from his helpful asides with regard to their particular situation. The church at large would also derive much blessing from his warm proclamation of the word of God. The world would certainly be better off because he would be out there with many others preaching the gospel and seeing men and women turn to faith in Jesus Christ. He would continue to blaze a trail for God in reaching the unreached with the life-giving message of Jesus and his love.

If he went ...

... he would be better off. He would be ushered immediately into the presence of the Lord whom he dearly loved. The trials and troubles of life would be gone. The tears of frustration would all be wiped away. The hassles and niggles of trying to work with so many people all of the time would end. The uncertainties about the future would evaporate as he entered heaven itself. The I-can't-do-all-that-I-want-to-do limitations imposed by time and circumstance would be forever removed as he walked through the pearly gates into glory. It would be heaven—and home—and his joy would be complete.

I have never seen it but I am told there is a headstone in a country churchyard in Montgomery, Alabama which reads:

Under the clover, and under the trees,
Here lies the body of Jonathan Pease.
Pease ain't here, only the pod,
Pease shelled out and went home to God.

1:25, 26

God's way is the best way

Paul reached the other side because the folks in Philippi were holding the ropes on his behalf—they faithfully prayed for him. Now when he finds himself at a T junction on the road of life, he hands the reins over to the Lord. The decision is the Lord's. It is better that way for his are a safe pair of hands. And when God makes the decision, success is guaranteed.

What was it? *Convinced (peithō) of this, I know (oida) that I will remain (menō), and I will continue with all of you for your progress (prokopē) and joy (chara) in the faith (pistis), so that through my being with you again your joy in Christ Jesus will overflow (perisseuō) on account of (en) me.*

There were lots of smiling faces when Paul announced he was staying for a wee while longer among them. Invariably, he was deliriously happy to go along with the plan of God for his life—he did not suffer from delusions of grandeur, he was only a tiny cog in God's giant wheel. Personal preferences were gladly set aside so that the sovereign purpose of God might be unfolded.

Basically, he wanted to go, but he was content to stay. For Paul, it was a classic win-win. Like the toss of a coin: heads I win, tails I win!

The baseline: God had a job for him to do. His work was not finished. Not yet, at any rate.

The things that happen unto me
Are not by chance, I know,
But because my Father's wisdom
Has willed to have it so.

For the furtherance of the gospel
As a part of his great plan,
God can use our disappointments
And the weaknesses of man.

Give me faith to meet them bravely,
Trials I do not understand,
To let God work his will in me—
To trust his guiding hand.
Help me to shine, a clear bright light,
And not to live in vain—
Help me hold forth the word of life
In triumph over pain.

1:27

A call to arms

Before Andrew Jackson became the seventh president of the United States of America, he served as a major-general in the Tennessee militia. During the War of 1812 his troops reached an all-time low in morale. A critical spirit grew up among them. They argued, bickered, and fought among themselves. It is reported that Old Hickory called them all together on one occasion when tensions were at their worst and told them: 'Gentlemen! Let's remember, the enemy is over there!'

In life, it is all about getting along with each other. We can polarise and pay the price or we can stick together and win the battle. We can be petty, fragment, and back a loser, or we can pull together in the same direction and back a winner.

All too often we forget the identity of the real enemy. He has confused us and sent us into disarray on a wild goose chase. We end up going round and round in circles like a dog chasing its tail. We sleep (even when we are on duty) and he edges forward. We fight among ourselves and he makes strident advances. We shoot our wounded and he smirks.

To me, the resounding challenge at the end of chapter one of Paul's letter is for God's people to head for the front line, get into the trenches, and fight. It is a call to arms.

We are soldiers in God's army, not Dad's army.

Paul reminds them *whether I come (erchomai) and see (horaō) you or only hear (akouō) about you in my absence (apeimi)* that he wants them to engage in the conflict of overpowering the enemy. He wants to see their age old adversary routed and roundly defeated. He knows only too well that if they give him an inch he will take more than a mile and, as a local fellowship, they are only one generation short of potential extinction. They are only one generation away from closing the doors. Yes, it is as urgent as that. Serious stuff.

Living Bibles

The emphasis in Paul's thinking is that we should be willing to stand up and be counted. He writes: *conduct yourselves (politeuomai) in a manner worthy (axiōs) of the gospel of Christ.* Paul is not playing the numbers game. Neither is he in the business of keeping the statisticians busy. But he is advocating a distinctive lifestyle for the people of God. We are meant to be different. Not odd!

Whether we like it or not, our lives speak volumes to those around us. Our actions speak louder than our words. Our lives are audible, hence the need for consistency. Someone once asked Gandhi: 'What is the greatest hindrance to Christian missions in India?' He replied: 'Christians!'

It has been well said that a man who refuses to stand for something will sooner or later fall for anything. That is why our personal conduct is a matter of mega importance. It is absolutely essential that there should be nothing in our lives that would cause the name of Christ to be smeared.

A godly life, a steady walk with the Lord, a bright testimony, a joy in the heart—all these prove to be a potent force in a corrupted world. A person of such ilk is a credit to his Saviour and a challenge to the sinner. It makes them sit up and think about what they are missing.

We are the Bibles the world is reading (*cf.* 2 Corinthians 3:2). I sometimes wonder, when they look at my life, what translation it is. A life consistently lived for Jesus is the greatest weapon we have against the enemy.

The finest sermon ever preached was titled: *The Life Lived.*

Let me make it personal and ask the searchingly pertinent question: 'What is the gospel according to you?'

You are writing a gospel,
A chapter each day,
By the deeds that you do
And the words that you say.
Men may read what you write,
Whether faithful or true:
Just what is the gospel
According to you?

United we stand

There is an intriguing phrase in Paul's letter which hits us between the eyes. It is when he says: *Whatever happens ... whether I come and see you or only hear about you ... I will know that you....* In one sense, he is laying it on the line by telling them that their behaviour should not be dependent on him. If he comes, they should be living a life that is glorifying to the Lord and, if he does not come, it should make no difference whatsoever. It should not be like the oft-quoted adage: when the cat's away the mice will play.

They had to learn to stand on their own two feet. It is all about striking a balance between independence and inter-dependence. We are on our own and yet we are in it together. Yes, we need each other in the family but, at the same time, we are expected to live our own lives to the glory of God.

Charles Swindoll, with a mix of realism and humour, says that '... so many live their lives too dependent on others. Such clinging vines draw most, if not all, of their energy from another. Not only is this unhealthy for the clinger, but it also drains too much energy from the clingee!' Enough said.

Team talk

Having cleared the air as to his position, Paul now moves up a gear when he tells them to *stand firm (histēmi) in one spirit (pneuma), contending (synathleō) as one (heis) man (psychē) for the faith of the gospel.* The stress here is on cooperation. The choice of words is highly suggestive for Paul speaks of them *contending as one man.* This is the Greek word from which we get our word 'athlete'. He sees the church as a team and he tactfully reminds them that it is teamwork that secures victories.

There are many players but there is only one team.

On the field of play we should be operating not against one another but for one another. We go forward hand in hand for the greater good of the gospel. We join hands and stand shoulder to shoulder as we engage the enemy in an eyeball to eyeball confrontation. United we stand. Victory is ensured.

The English novelist Rudyard Kipling penned a verse that visualises this:

Now this is the law of the jungle
As old and as true as the sky;
And the wolf that keep it may prosper,
And the wolf that shall break it must die.
As the creeper that girdles the tree trunk,
The law runneth forward and back—
And the strength of the pack is the wolf,
And the strength of the wolf is the pack.

To put it simply: the strength of the church is the Christian and the strength of the Christian is the church. John Wesley declared on one memorable occasion: 'If I had three hundred men who feared nothing but God, hated nothing but sin, and were determined to know nothing among men save Jesus Christ and him crucified, I would set the world on fire!'

One of Aesop's fables is about a father who had seven sons. To each son he gave a stick. Each was asked to break his stick. No problem there, it was easily done. Then the father took another seven sticks and bound them together. He then asked the seven sons to break the sticks. Not one of them could break the sticks which had been bound together as one.

Failure to pull (and play) together will ensure that the church goes into the hands of the receiver. It will hasten her demise and her days of usefulness will become a thing of the past.

1:28

Not so friendly fire

There are always casualties on the field of battle. That is part of the price that has to be paid. Suffering is inevitable for those who would be soldiers in the army of the Lord. It is not a question of *if* it comes, but *when* it comes. We should expect it and be willing to share in it. When we face it square on, then our confidence will grow.

The ups and downs of life should make us better, not bitter.

Our spiritual muscle will be so much stronger and our faith will have a lot more clout in the market place. It will give us street credibility.

Horseplay

Paul warned the Philippians not to be *frightened (ptyrō) in any way by those who oppose (antikeimai) [them]*. The natural inclination is to run scared. The word Paul used here is of a horse shying away from battle or of horses that were so terrified they went into an uncontrollable stampede. That only happens when fear gets the upper hand. The tendency then is to quickly click our heels and not be seen for dust.

It is worth noting that this is the only place in the New Testament where this particular word is used and it is very appropriate for the little group of believers living in Philippi during a violent period of history. It is more than coincidental that Paul addresses them in the manner which he does. It is a touch of inspirational genius.

This 'courage, brother, do not stumble' attitude in the face of such ruthless oppression and concentrated opposition has a double compensation allied to it. It is a token of their salvation and of their enemies doom: *This is a sign (endeixis) to them that they will be destroyed (apōleia), but that you will be saved (sōtēria)—and that by God.*

The sheer inability of their avowed enemies to intimidate them becomes proof of the genuineness of their faith in the Lord. It gives to the casual onlooker and interested spectator an appreciation of what it costs to be a Christian. We do not go looking or spoiling for a fight but neither do we run away from it if it happens. It proves beyond any shadow of doubt that our faith is real, we are real, and our God is real.

1:29

Persecution complex

Paul then adds another dimension to it when he says that *it has been granted (charizomai) to you on behalf (hyper) of Christ not only to believe (pisteuō) on him, but also to suffer (paschō) for him.* It is patently obvious that believing is the delightful part, suffering is the difficult part. Believing is relatively easy, suffering is intensely hard.

- Who likes being persecuted?
- Who enjoys facing times of hardship and deprivation?
- Who relishes and looks forward with glee to moments of pain and trauma?
- Who gets excited if they have to face times of severe trial and testing?

Probably none of us! And yet Paul indicates that when we suffer in the will of God we are doing it for the Lord. It is something which he has *granted* to us—we are to see it as a love gift from the Lord. We should, therefore, accept it with an overwhelming sense of privilege realising that he knows what is best for us. It is a rare honour conferred only on those whom he can trust with such an expression of his love.

1:30

Been there, done that

In a final word of encouragement, Paul reminds them that they are not alone in their conflict for he is going through something very similar. He writes: *since you are going through the same struggle (agōn) you saw I had, and now hear that I still have.* The Greek word translated *struggle* is the term from which we get our word 'agony'. Agony is agony, pure and simple.

It is the identical word that is used in reference to the Lord's critical hour in the Garden of Gethsemane (*cf.* Luke 22:44). Life is not a playground, it is a battlefield. God promised us a safe landing not a smooth sailing.

That means Jesus knows exactly what they are going through and he can empathise with them. Paul sports the tee shirt 'been there, done that', he can sit where they sit, he can put his arms around their sagging shoulders and say: 'I really do understand because I'm going through the same!' They are not alone. And when it comes to your front door and mine, we are not on our own either.

In the early days of Christianity, a scoffer once enquired: 'What is your Carpenter doing now?' And the answer of the unperturbed Christian was bold: 'Making a coffin for your Emperor!'

At times it may appear as though the Lord is like Scotch tape: we cannot see him, but we know he is there!

Invisible. Sometimes! Invincible. Always! We really are in the best of company. Cheer up!

2

No Saviour like God's Son

Attitude matters

Stripped naked, falsely accused, humiliated beneath the glare of the lights and the stare of the Gestapo, Victor Frankl stood shaved and shivering in a Nazi courtroom. His shorn head was a symbol of his shorn life—they had stolen his home, his freedom, his possessions, and had even killed his family.

Yet as Frankl, a Viennese Jew, faced the men who had robbed him of everything and left him with only years of indignity ahead, he realised there was one thing they could never take away.

His choice of attitude!

He could choose despair or hope, bitterness or forgiveness. He could choose to wallow in self-pity or to endure. The quality of his outer life was ruthlessly beaten into submission, but his inner life was his to rule.

It is all down to our attitude and how we handle what life throws at us.

'What lies behind us and what lies before us are tiny matters compared to what lies within us.' (Ralph Waldo Emerson)

One string to our bow

Another man illustrates the importance of attitude differently—Niccolo Paganini, the gifted Italian composer and concert violinist. One night, performing before a full house, he began to play a particularly difficult concerto. The audience sat in rapt attention. Suddenly, one of the strings on his Stradivarius snapped, and dangled uselessly beneath his bow.

Perspiration beaded his forehead. The maestro frowned. But he continued to play, his genius lending beauty to his improvisation. But then, unbelievably, a second string broke! And then a third! Only a single string remained taut, but the great musician finished the piece.

His final notes were swallowed in the wild applause of the appreciative audience. As they sank back into their seats, he waved them to silence. With a twinkle in his eye, he shouted: 'Paganini ... and one string!' Then he lifted his violin and began his encore as the audience shook their heads in utter amazement. It was a touch surreal.

It's the thought that counts

Again, it is the attitude factor that makes all the difference. He could have gone to pieces and wrecked the performance or carry on as he did with gusto as if nothing had happened.

I came across the two quite different stories outlined above as I was making preparation for this particular chapter. They are a superb illustration of what it takes to be successful in this life, even when we are down to our last string.

Like our friend Paganini we need to rediscover that our strength is not in the number of strings on our violin, but in the tune we are playing. Yes, it is true, our circumstances are not always under our control, but our attitudes always are—it is up to us to choose how we think.

W. Clement Stone expressed it like this: 'There is little difference in people, but that little difference makes a big difference. The little difference is attitude. The big difference is whether it is positive or negative.'

'Life is 10 percent what happens to us and 90 percent how we react to what happens.' (Charles Swindoll)

The right fist of fellowship

Without doubt, this was a timely message to the Philippian church. On the whole they were a fairly peaceful and happy group, but apparently there were rumblings going on behind closed doors. From reading between the lines it would seem there were a couple of personality clashes. There were some strained relationships and these were affecting the unity of the fellowship. The lovely feeling of close harmony which they previously enjoyed was slowly but surely evaporating.

There was friction in the assembly, something was just not quite right. Feelings were frayed. They were suffering from wear and tear.

Christians are like porcupines! They have many good points, but they are hard to get close to. The main reason is their prickly personalities keep needling each other.

Grasping the nettle

In Paul's favour, he is not afraid to do that. It is a perennial problem and, when it gets out of hand, it can be an eyesore. So he reminds them of the beauty and blessings of unity—the gospel's hallmark. Be positive. Do not be negative in your outlook.

As a church they had so much going for them, they were a delightful group of people. It was a super fellowship to belong to, it was thriving. Yet the red warning lights were flashing. The smoke signals indicated the presence of a fire. There was something smouldering—a hot potato.

Paul hit the nail on the head, he put his finger squarely on the problem. Disunity. There was a ripple on the water, a kind of undercurrent. This particular problem is not exclusive to the saints at Philippi. Sadly, across the broad acres of planet earth there are many similar situations. Depressing. It can be.

The astute Mark Twain said: 'I built a cage and in it I put a dog and a cat. After a little training, I got the dog and cat to the point where they lived peaceably together. Then I introduced a pig, a goat, a kangaroo, some birds, and a monkey. It took a bit of time but, after a few adjustments, they learned to live in harmony together. So encouraged was I by such success that I added a Presbyterian, a Jew, a Muslim, along with a Baptist missionary that I captured on the same trip. And in a very short time, there wasn't a single living thing left in my cage!'

At home and abroad so many of God's people are not getting along with each other. We see it in local companies of believers, we see it on mission stations dotted across the world. This is an area of major concern to spiritually sensitive believers—incompatibility. Some people just cannot get on with other people. They are inconsonant. Mismatches. It does not say much for the unity of the body of Christ.

Many churches are like the cartoon once featured in *Leadership* journal that showed two sections of a congregation sitting with their backs to one another and each facing a sidewall. The preacher is in the pulpit and is heard to say: 'It's come to my attention that there's been a split in the church!'

2:1

Unity in diversity

Paul's impassioned plea is for unity, not uniformity. There is a subtle difference between them. Uniformity is the result of pressure from without—it is when people want us to conform to their way of doing things. They say: 'Be like me and do it my way!' We dress alike, look alike, sound alike, think alike, act alike—when that happens, we become spiritual clones.

On the other hand, unity comes from within and is a matter for the heart. It is best experienced when we are conformed to the image of Jesus Christ. He says: 'Be like me and do it my way!' It means to be on the same team, going for the same goals, for the benefit of one another.

We are different. And we are meant to be. But we can still be one. We will have our multifarious opinions, our pet likes and dislikes, sure we will, but that does not mean we are not one in heart and soul. There is unity in diversity. We are not a group of automatons walking in lockstep with one another—we are individuals who, despite our differences and idiosyncrasies, are willing to show love and respect for one another.

Others

In chapter one, Paul talked about the place he was in; here, in chapter two, he focuses on the people he is with. Earlier he stressed the need to have a single mind, now he recommends we have a submissive mind—that is, we will have and hold the mind of Christ. Formerly, Paul was in the groove of the soul winner, here he is in the mould of a servant.

That, says Paul, is the way forward. We need to see ourselves as nothing more than servants, nothing less than servants, and nothing else but servants. It is all about the attitude of servanthood, a keen willingness to serve others.

Others, Lord! Yes, others!
Let this my motto be.
Help me to live for others,
That I may live for thee.

There are people with whom we immediately feel at home, we relate to them easily, we have an instant rapport with them, we just enjoy being in their company. Great! However, there are those with whom we have a difficult relationship, they rub us up the wrong way, they tramp on our toes especially the ones with corns, we find it so hard to relax when they are within earshot.

Welcome to the real world! Such is life in evangelicalism. Nevertheless, Paul challenges us to pull out all the stops and cause the dulcet tones of harmony to pervade the atmosphere again. It will be like music to the ear and it would *make his joy complete (plēroō)* (2:2).

Getting our act together

Paul says: 'Look, see what you have! Look again, see what you are!' In a deft touch, he gives to the Christians a fourfold incentive to pull together: *If you have any encouragement (paraklēsis) from being united with Christ, if any comfort (paramythion) from his love (agapē), if any fellowship (koinōnia) with the Spirit, if any tenderness (splanchnon) and compassion (oiktirmos).*

Here is a quartet of pointers to set them back on the straight and narrow. They have one feature in common—they all begin with *if*. In the Greek construction, it may be better and wiser to translate the phrase with the word 'since'. What are they?

- We have union with Christ—our encouragement.
- We are the recipients of his love—our enjoyment.
- We have life in the Spirit—our endowment.
- We have felt his heartbeat—our endearment.

Paul's valiant and vigorous appeal for unity is based not on their potentially shaky feelings about the family, but on the unshakeable facts of their faith. These are viable and sustainable reasons for Christian unity among God's people.

William Hendriksen in his *Geneva Series Commentary* summarises it in a most helpful manner when he writes: 'The main thrust of what the apostle is saying is this—if then you receive any help or encouragement or comfort from your vital union with Christ, and if the love of Christ toward you does at all provide you with an incentive for action; if, moreover, you are at all rejoicing in the marvellous Spirit fellowship and if you have any experience of the tender mercy and compassion of Christ, then prove your gratitude for all this by loving your brothers and sisters at home.'

2:2

Esprit de corps

Paul says: 'This is what you have received, now, share it and show it to others!' For him, living back in Rome this would be the icing on the cake. It would really turn his day into a red-letter day. Like C S Lewis, he would be 'surprised by joy' and his cup would be full and running over. What a prayer. What an aspiration. All he wanted was for them to be united, that is all.

The animated apostle, with verve, appeals to them:

- 'Do it for my sake,

- do it for the Lord's sake, and
- do it for your own sake!'

They were to be *like-minded (autos ho phroneō)*. This is a reference to what they believed—it is talking about doctrine and the great tenets of our faith. They were to sign on the same dotted line giving assent to the fundamentals of the faith.

There is no spiritual unity without doctrinal oneness.

A T Robertson in his *Word Pictures* has noted that, when it comes to the basis of our faith, Christians should be 'like clocks that strike at the same moment.' The foundation for their unity is the word of God—truth unchanged, unchanging.

They were to *[have] the same (autos) love (agapē)*. One in heart. They were to have the same love—not loving the same things but possessing the same love. It is imperative that we show to others that the love of God is flowing in us and through us. Ted Rendell grasped this idea well when he wrote that 'love always comes to visibility.'

Paul also longed for them to be *one (heis) in spirit (sympsychos) and purpose (phroneō)*. It is a most unusual phrase that Paul has coined here for it really conveys the idea of having 'joint souls'. We are to be soul brothers, in harmony with all of God's people.

Essentially, Paul is saying: 'If you want all these things, you can have them, but you'll need to change your attitude and become of one mind! The choice is yours!'

2:3, 4

Unhealthy ambition

Paul is not pussy-footing when he moves into this section. He tells it like it is. He spells out the danger of the 'me, myself, and I' philosophy and, at the same time, he knocks the 'grab all you can get' attitude that seems to permeate so much of our thinking in today's world. It is a dog-eat-dog world out there and the puppies do not survive! We are told if we want to survive that we will need to hold on to the ladder we are climbing for dear life—to succeed, we are advised to claw our way to the top.

Paul says we are to *do nothing (mēdeis) out of selfish ambition (eritheia) or vain conceit (kenodoxia)*. What a challenge! He is prohibiting a competitive selfish spirit within the church of Jesus Christ. Sadly this attitude is behind many of the petty squabbles we see in our churches, it is people determined to get their own way so that they can do their own thing. It is riding roughshod over other people. It is a seriously unhealthy passion to look after number one. I heard of two little boys who were riding on a hobbyhorse. One of them said: 'If one of us would get off, then I could ride better!'

Watchman Nee, the Chinese evangelist, tells of a Christian he once knew in China. He was a poor rice farmer and his fields lay high on a mountain. Every day he pumped water into the paddies of new rice, and every morning he returned to find that a neighbour who lived down the hill had opened the dykes surrounding the Christian's field to let the water fill his own.

For a while the Christian ignored the injustice, but at last he became desperate. He met and prayed with other Christians and came up with this solution. The next day the Christian farmer rose early in the morning and first filled his neighbour's fields, then he attended his own. Watchman Nee tells how the neighbour subsequently became a Christian—his unbelief overcome by a genuine demonstration of a Christian's humility and Christ-like character.

Nothing from ear to ear

Conceit means 'an empty glory'. There is nothing to it, there is nothing in it. It speaks of an over-inflated self image. Big head, large ego! A visitor arrived a little late for the Sunday morning guest service in a mega church. Not wanting to rush into the main sanctuary, she waited in the vestibule until it was an appropriate moment to enter. After listening to the preacher for a few minutes, she asked an usher: 'Who's that preaching this morning?' 'I don't know,' the usher replied, 'but he sure does recommend himself highly!'

Conceit is like a balloon—the larger it stretches on the outside, the bigger the emptiness inside.

To change the analogy, it is like the empty can that makes the most noise! You see, there are none so empty as those who are full of themselves. John Wooden, former coach of the UCLA Bruins basketball team gives this helpful advice:

- Talent is God given—be humble.
- Fame is man given—be thankful.
- Conceit is self given—be careful.

Humble and proud of it!

During a time of severe economic recession, a baker sent for twenty of the poorest children in town. He pointed to a basket of freshly baked loaves. Each child was to help themselves to one. They were also to come back every day at the same time for another loaf and keep doing it until the economy picked up.

The children began to push and shove, rummaging through the wicker basket for the biggest loaves. They ran off without so much as a word of thanks. One little girl waited until all the others had finished, then she picked up the small loaf that was left, thanked the old man kindly, and went home.

The next day it was a repeat performance. When the little girl got home that day and her mother began to cut into the loaf she found a pile of shiny silver coins inside. Immediately, she sent her daughter back to the baker with the money. 'No, my child, it was not a mistake,' he said. 'I had the coins put into the smallest loaf to reward you!' The greatest achievements in life are those that benefit others.

The key to unity among the Christian family is to have a spirit of humility. A diamond facet in being truly human. Paul underlines this when he writes: ... *in humility (tapeinophrosynē) consider (hēgeomai) others (allēlōn) better (hyperechō) than yourselves. Each (hekastos) of you should look (skopeō) not only to your own interests, but also to the interests of others.*

Andrew Murray is credited with this definition: 'The humble person is not one who thinks meanly of himself. He simply does not think of himself at all.' John Stott calls humility 'that rarest and fairest of Christian virtues.' Humility is a grace that when you think you have it, you have lost it. If you are humble, you do not write a book on how humble you are, with twelve life-size pictures in it. When Augustine was asked to list the three central principles of the Christian life, he replied: 'One, humility. Two, humility. Three, humility.'

A humble person is someone who accepts himself for who he is, he is someone who is grateful to God for all that he has done for him, he is an individual who rightly assesses the value of the gifts that the Holy Spirit has given to him. He will not overestimate himself and thereby fall into the snare of pride. Neither will he underestimate himself and be caught in the trap of a false humility. His will be a balanced outlook, a Christ-like attitude.

'The greatest men are those who are humble before God and the tallest men are those who bend before God.' (Richard Halverson)

A humble person is people orientated. There will be a willingness and desire to invest himself in the lives of others and go beyond the second mile. People will matter to him, not for what he can get out of them or impart to them, but for who they are. The individual is important in his thinking and in his planning.

It seems to me when we do what the apostle is asking us to do that we will be in a better position to experience the thrill of oneness in the church of Christ. Unity is available. And attainable. How? By adopting the right attitude.

It is when we extend to our brothers and sisters in the family of God the right hand of fellowship, not the right fist of fellowship. Maybe we need to link our hearts together a little more instead of banging our heads together. To be united is infinitely better than being untied.

2:5

The way up is down!

'Few things are harder to put up with than the annoyance of a good example.' (Mark Twain)

A good example. The seventeenth-century Puritan Thomas Brooks wisely observed that 'example is the most powerful rhetoric.' We need look no further than Jesus. That is the gist of what Paul says: *Your attitude (phroneō) should be the same as that of Christ Jesus.* He is an example par excellence of a totally unselfish outlook. Jesus said an emphatic 'No' to everything that might have been advantageous to self.

'When he came among us he did not dazzle us with displays of overwhelming divine power nor did he intimidate us with bullying tactics,' observes Philip Greenslade. His smashingly beautiful attitude is such that it automatically puts him in the category of the ideal role model. Exemplary. Incomparable. Unprecedented. Because of that, his is a mindset and lifestyle worth embracing and emulating. A top-notch paradigm.

What did Jesus do? He came down from heaven to earth in the greatest stoop of all time. Jesus bucked the trend when he put his foot on the ladder and stepped down, one rung at a time. Others want to climb up the ladder. Not Jesus! He climbed down! And met us at our own level.

* He left the splendour of heaven.
* He made himself nothing.
* He took the nature of a servant.
* He was made in the likeness of humanity.
* He humbled himself.
* He became obedient to death.
* He died on a cross.

This is what submission is all about. It is an experience of Calvary in the life of the Christian. It is as personal as it can be and as life-changing as it should be.

You came from heaven to earth
To show the way,
From the earth to the cross
My debt to pay;
From the cross to the grave,
From the grave to the sky,
Lord, I lift your name on high.

My heart was moved when I read the words penned by Charles Swindoll in relation to this supreme act of humility and servanthood. He said: 'Rather than lobbying for his right to remain in heaven and continuing to enjoy all the benefits of that exalted role as the second member of the Godhead and Lord of the created world, he willingly said yes. He agreed to cooperate with a plan that would require his releasing ecstasy and accepting agony. In a state of absolute perfection and undiminished deity, he willingly came to earth.

'Leaving the angelic hosts who flooded his presence with adoring praise, he unselfishly accepted a role that would require his being misunderstood, abused, cursed, and crucified. He unhesitatingly surrendered the fellowship and protection of the Father's glory for the lonely path of obedience and torturous death.'

Jesus did it all!

- For you.
- For them.
- For me.

If we are staggered with his condescension in 2:5-8, then we are bowled over with his coronation in 2:9-11. His descent from glory is recorded prior to his ascent to the throne. The abiding principle that should dictate our thinking is enshrined in the example of Jesus: the way up is down (*cf.* James 4:10).

This exquisite portion in Paul's letter to the Philippians—the great parabola of Scripture—was probably a credal statement used by the early church. It may even have been a hymn that was sung when the Lord's people were gathered together in his name. It is a brilliantly superb masterpiece of Christology which focuses exclusively on the person and work of the Lord Jesus—an impressively rich and unusual combination of meekness and majesty.

The story of the cross is recorded in the Gospel narratives and is suitably explained in the Epistles; this, however, is the only place where we are given an insight into what Calvary meant to him. We see the cross from the perspective of Jesus and through his eyes. We tread, therefore, on very holy ground indeed. 'We do well to remember that this privilege is given to us not to satisfy our curiosity,' writes J A Motyer, 'but to reform our lives.'

In order to feel the pulse of this truly remarkable section, I want us to look at the steps that Jesus took as he made the round trip from glory to glory. David Jeremiah of *Turning Point Ministries* has a skilfully worded, alliterative outline for these few verses:

- Step 1: he relinquished his place.
- Step 2: he refused his prerogative.
- Step 3: he renounced his privileges.
- Step 4: he restricted his presence.
- Step 5: he realised his purpose.
- Step 6: he received his promotion.

What are the key phrases that help us open the door into the mind of Christ? What was it that seemed important to Jesus? What principles did he cherish? Let us try to discover what made him tick.

2:6

The Servant King

We are confronted with the reality of his deity when we read: *who, being (hyparchō) in very nature (morphē) God.* This is the awesome place of prominence which Christ enjoyed. He and God are one—co-equal, co-eternal, and co-essential—this is Jesus before Bethlehem. What one has the other has. What one is the other is.

Jesus is God through and through.

He is all God. He is God. There is not the tiniest fraction of him that is not divine. All that God is, Jesus Christ was, is, and ever will be.

Paul continues in the same vein when he informs us that he *did not consider (hēgeomai) equality (isos) with God something to be grasped (harpagmos).* In other words, what Jesus claimed to be was not something he had pilfered or stolen. What he said about himself was not gained by false pretences. He is equal with the Father.

Even though he was God and enjoyed such a favoured position with all its rights and honours, he refused to cling on to these, he was willing to give them up for a season. That is the message of Christ, the Servant King. He surrendered that which he loved in order that he might serve those whom he loved.

2:7

Nothing

The phrase *made himself nothing (kenoō)* can be translated 'he emptied himself' or 'he made himself of no reputation'. Jesus certainly never emptied himself of his deity, he was still God at the incarnation. There were many instances in his life and ministry when he showed his divine attributes in the realm of the miraculous.

Jesus became what he never was before, yet he never ceased to be what he is eternally.

It simply means that he laid aside certain rights that were his. He forfeited many of the privileges which were enjoyed by him in the glory. In emptying himself, he voluntarily stepped from being a Son of the Father in heaven to being the Son of Man on earth.

That meant him *taking (lambanō) the very nature of a servant (doulos)*. It is instructive to realise that the same word *nature* is used both here and in the preceding verse. The one who was in the form of God took upon himself the form of a servant. Jesus was happy to take the place and position of a slave—the sovereign assumed the status of a servant both in nature and by practice. This was the defining moment when omnipotence surrendered to impotence.

As God, Christ owned everything, but when he became a servant, he borrowed everything—a place to be born, a pillow to lay his head, a boat to journey in, a pulpit to preach from, an animal to ride into a city, a room for the Passover meal, and a tomb in which to be buried.

Jesus was also *made in human (anthrōpos) likeness (homoiōma)*. The word *likeness* suggests similarity but difference. Though his humanity was genuine, he was different from all other humans in that he was sinless. He was identified with sinners because he had all the essential attributes of humanity.

Jesus was more than God in a body.

He became the God man. He was fully God and fully man. He had the same flesh and blood that we have, he knew the limitations of life down here, he was aware of the ups and downs of this life and was subject to all the emotions that mankind faces.

2:8

Crucified

Nothing could be more cruel than death on a cross. A person who was crucified is said to have died a thousand deaths before finally dying. Jesus was willing to go through with such an excruciating and shameful crucifixion so that we might be set free from the shackles and bondage of sin. Charles Wesley (1707-88) put it justly when he wrote:

'Tis mystery all! The immortal dies!

We read that *being found in appearance (schēma) as a man (anthrōpos), he humbled (tapeinoō) himself and became obedient (hypēkoos) to death—even death (thanatos) on a cross (stauros)!* Jesus lived his life in the shadow of the cross. From start to finish, it was a path of humiliation. This was all part of the Father's plan for the cross was no accident or afterthought. It was central to the unfolding drama of redemption as revealed in the word of God.

Athanasius (c.296-373), Bishop of Alexandria, noted that crucifixion was the only death a man can die with arms outstretched. He said that Jesus died like that to invite people of all nations and all generations to come to him.

During some unsettled days in ancient Rome, a slave heard that his master's name was on the liquidation list. He quickly put on his master's coat and quietly awaited the arrival of the political butchers. When they found the slave dressed in his master's clothing, they killed him, supposing him to be the master. Likewise, the Master of the universe, Jesus Christ, took on himself the cloak of our humanity. The death he endured is the death we deserved and, through his death, we have been spared.

When reflecting on the cross, E H Swinstead was moved to pen these words:

> *Though he was rich, so rich,*
> *Yet for our sakes how poor he became!*
> *Even his garments they parted*
> *When he hung on the cross of shame.*
> *All that he had he gave for me,*
> *That I might be rich through eternity.*

2:9a

First Ascension Day

Jesus is where he is today because God placed him there, he is what he is because God planned it that way—*therefore (dio) God exalted him to the highest place (hyperypsoō).* Because of what he did, God moved and did his bit, he exalted Jesus. From out of the deepest depths to the loftiest heights. From the gutters of earth to the glories of eternity. Jesus Christ is the only corpse in history who outlived his pallbearers.

- Up from the tomb in wondrous resurrection!
- Up through the skies in glorious ascension!
- Up to the throne in illustrious session!

No higher place could be given to him for, in the Father's eyes, he is the highest of all. He has exalted him far above all. He is on the top rung of the ladder, he has scaled the summit, he has reached the zenith. The Father welcomed him back with wide-open arms. As the Lord walked along the pavement of heaven the applause from the angelic band was rapturous and spontaneous.

When we speak of his exaltation, we include his resurrection, ascension, and coronation. He has sat down at the Father's right hand, hailed as a Prince and a Saviour. For him the crowning day has happened! At his exaltation he received back from the Father all that he set aside when he came to earth; in fact, he was able to enter into a whole new dimension of ministry as our Great High Priest.

This is 'the glory of the battle scarred hero whose scars are his crown.' (A T Robertson)

2:9b-11

Jesus is King

... and gave him the name (onoma) that is above (hyper) every name, that at the name of Jesus every knee (gony) should bow (kamptō) in heaven (epouranios) and on earth (epigeios) and under the earth (katachthonios), and every tongue (glōssa) confess (exomologeō) that Jesus Christ is Lord, to the glory (doxa) of God the Father.

J. Dwight Pentecost explains that the word 'name' is used here in its Old Testament sense where the name represents the total person. It speaks of the office, the rank, and the dignity attached to the person because of his position. This name is incomparable, the superlative of superlatives. Paul is anticipating a future day when men will bend the knee at the mention of Jesus' name, a moment when they will confess that *Jesus Christ is Lord.* At the appropriate hour, all the good angels, plus the redeemed from every age, will bow before the Lord. Similarly, every inhabitant living on planet earth will bow. And all those under the earth—that is, all those populating hell together with the fallen evil angels—will also be required to bow before the glorious Lord.

On that day the cycle will be completed. He will have gone full circle. The one who was humiliated will then be exalted. The one who was brought so low will then be raised up on high. We will see God resplendent in his full colours for *Jesus shall take the highest honour [and the] highest praise.*

Graham Kendrick composed a song based on these verses:

Meekness and majesty,
Manhood and deity,
In perfect harmony,
The man who is God:
Lord of eternity
Dwells in humanity,
Kneels in humility
And washes our feet.

Father's pure radiance,
Perfect in innocence,
Yet learns obedience
To death on a cross:
Suffering to give us life,
Conquering through sacrifice;
And, as they crucify,
Prays 'Father, forgive.'

Wisdom unsearchable,
God the invisible,
Love indestructible
In frailty appears.
Lord of infinity,
Stooping so tenderly,
Lifts our humanity
To the heights of his throne.

O, what a mystery,
Meekness and majesty:
Bow down and worship,
For this is your God,
This is your God!

Charles Lamb, the essayist, once said: 'If Shakespeare walked into the room, we would stand. But if Jesus Christ walked into the room, we would bow!' Jesus is Lord!

2:12

He works in, we work out

What a chapter it has been so far: an impassioned appeal for unity, a lovely example of an early Christian hymn or poem, a noble declaration on the Lordship of Jesus Christ, a profound illustration of unsurpassed excellence on the person and work of Jesus—all in the space of eleven verses—and the end is not yet!

Paul has been showing us that the road to *happiness* is one where there is a real sense of unity in the family of God. As believers, we are to engage our hearts in the pursuit of *humility* by following in the footsteps of Jesus when he became a servant. The end of that journey will take us to a place of *honour* when God will exalt us in his own good time. Now, he reminds us in verses 12-18 that the great goal in the life of the Christian should be that of *holiness*.

In the previous section we saw the pre-eminence of Jesus Christ. He is supreme in life, in death, in resurrection, and in glory. He is extraordinarily second to none. He stands head and shoulders above all his would-be rivals. Unexcelled. In reality, none can be seriously compared to him.

There is no real pretender waiting in the wings to take his throne.

Having said that, the apostle leaves us in no doubt that it is our salient responsibility to have an attitude akin to his. He has described for us the mind of Christ. Presently, he directs our interest to the dynamics of that same mind.

Yes, we read about it, we agree with it, we nod our heads in approval, we admire with spellbound eyes the example of Jesus, we are inspired by all that he has done—but how do we get it? That is the crunch question.

Jesus Christ is the pattern we wish to copy. But he is more. He also provides us with the power to make sure it becomes a reality in our lives. He will equip and enable us by his Spirit. He gives us not only the ability to keep our heads above water but to swim freely in the water. As Warren Wiersbe explains: 'It is not by imitation, but by incarnation' that we are able to share the secrets of the mind of Christ. He did it. With his help, so can we.

We will discover that the Christian life is not, therefore, a series of 'ups and downs' but an ongoing process of 'ins and outs'. That means, God works *in* and we work *out*. Perhaps we should stick a label on every Christian: 'Danger—God at work!'

Getting connected

The opening word *therefore (hōste)* is the unavoidable link between what has gone before and what is following after. It forges a join with all that has been said and what he is just about to say. The two are intertwined. One follows hard on the heels of the other. God's 'therefore' in verse 9 is matched by the Christian's *therefore* in this verse.

J A Motyer makes the interesting comment that 'there is always a blessing to be had from the word "therefore" in the Bible.' I must say I have never heard it put that way before—however, my old Bible Class teacher (Harry Mallon) used to say: 'When you see the word "therefore" in the Bible, you stop and ask yourself the question, what's it there for?'

In this instance, the reason is plain for all to see. We say: 'Jesus is our reason for living.' Paul says: 'Fine, right here, he is your recipe for life.' We have seen an outstanding example of someone who held nothing back—Jesus has shown us the way to do it; now, says Paul, the shoe is on the other foot, it is your turn to put it into practice—adopt the Nike philosophy, just go and do it.

Christ was obedient in death, we must be obedient in life.

Martin Luther defined the situation neatly: 'Good works do not make a good man, but a good man does good works.'

It is imperative we remember that Paul is writing here to those who are already members of God's global family. That is why he calls them *my dear friends (agapētos)*. These words have nothing to do with his readers becoming Christians, they already are.

Work out!

They were not to work for their own salvation since that is a gift from God. They were to work at it, hence the comment: *continue to work out (katergazomai) your salvation (sōtēria) with fear (phobos) and trembling (tromos)*. If you like, they were to stop playing church and be zealously committed to the cause of Christ. They were to be sold out to Jesus.

It was a stirring challenge for them to live out their faith in the rough and tumble of everyday life and, by so doing, impact their community for Jesus. He was exhorting them to get up out of their soft grandstand seats and get down to the pitch where the action was. The particular brand of Christianity advocated by Paul is one where we get our feet wet.

God is not looking for smooth clean hands, he wants dirty hands.

The phrase *work out* incorporates the idea of working something through to its full completion such as we do when solving a mathematical problem. It was also used to describe those who worked in the mines, they would work it so as to reclaim the maximum amount possible. The term was also used in the farming context for a farmer would work a field so as to secure the greatest harvest possible. It is all about achieving and exploiting the potential that is there. And being serious in the quest for such a benefit.

Paul says: 'You have been given a stockpile of resources, like nobody's business, now go out and realise the full capacity of all that you are and have in Jesus Christ.'

He longs that we might lead fulfilled lives and be at our best for God. He desires nothing more than we maintain our spiritual glow and be at our peak for him. He is looking for dedicated followers who will be spiritual fitness fanatics—people willing to fight the spiritual flab.

Discipline is essential. It is indispensable and vital. There are no shortcuts. There is no easy 1-2-3 course to adopt. It is a matter of working at it and working it out.

A daily workout producing pints of spiritual sweat will ensure a leaner, fitter—and healthier—Christian.

2:13

God's apprenticeship scheme

For it is God who works in (energeō) you to will (thelō) and to act (energeō) according to his good purpose (eudokia). This is marvellous because it tells me that God is actively working in us—a principle as old as the hills. I think of Moses whose dream to be a leader in Egypt was smashed when he identified with his own people and stupidly killed an Egyptian. Banished to Midian, he became a shepherd, an occupation loathsome to the Egyptians (*cf.* Genesis 46:34).

Surely this was a source of immense frustration to him. He was highly trained in hieroglyphics, chemistry, mathematics, and astronomy, and now he had to set all these skills aside to do a job which he has been taught is detestable. Talk about someone over-qualified for a position!

Moses discovered, however, that there are certain life-building lessons that cannot be learned in a palace. Some can only be learned in a desert. With that in mind, he spent forty years in the back of beyond looking after a flock of sheep before God used him to lead the fledgling nation of Israel out of the land of Egypt. Those were days of preparation when God was moulding and shaping the life of his servant. Moses did not know it, but this was Philippians 2:13 in action.

Who I am is more important than what I do

God is more interested in the man than he is in the ministry.

He is more concerned about the workman than he is about the work. That is the prime reason why the Lord chooses to work in us before operating through us.

Why do we obey him? It should not be in response to pressure from the outside but from a power on the inside. It is *God ... in you.* That is the entrance of God into our lives. Why does he bother doing it? It is *according to his good purpose.* That reminds me of his enjoyment for God does it because he wants to do it. How does he accomplish it? It is because he *works in you.* Surely that indicates the boundless energy of God.

There are two little phrases of two words that are used to describe what God does: *to will* and *to act.* Both the desire and the deed belong to God. Both the prompting and the performing are attributed to him.

Back to square one

We are almost back to where we started—God works in and we work out! It is a joint initiative. A partnership. A shared program of activity. In that sense, we respond to what he has done. I chuckled when I came across a story that illustrates this truth rather well.

It is the tale of a country farmer who was visited by his new, fresh-faced pastor. As the pastor surveyed the farm for the first time, he commented: *'John, this is a great farm you and God have!'* *'Thank you,'* said John, *'but you should have been here five years ago and seen it when God had it all by himself!'*

Ouch! But the lesson is clear. God works through us. He will not do for us what we should be doing for ourselves. It is only as we cooperate with him that we see the true potential of our lives realised.

2:14, 15

Shine bright

The light always shines brightest where and when it is darkest. Several years ago the mayor of Toronto launched a campaign called *Light the*

Night. The idea was for residents to leave their lights burning overnight in order to discourage crime and unsociable behaviour. Our world is inky black, our society is muddy and murky. 'We are all like the moon. We have a dark side we don't want anybody to see,' notes Mark Twain.

Hence the need of the hour is for us to give careful heed to Paul: *Do everything without complaining (gongysmos) or arguing (dialogismos), so that you may become blameless (amemptos) and pure (akeraios), children (teknon) of God without fault (amōmos) in a crooked (skolios) and depraved (diastrephō) generation (genea), in which you shine (phainō) like stars (phōstēr) in the universe (kosmos).*

Every believer—in every city, country, and continent—is to be involved in God's current 'light the night' campaign.

Lights out

These opening words 'come like a shock of cold on a hot day' writes J A Motyer. In other words, if we fail to get a grip on our attitude, it will manifest itself in two ways—*complaining* and *arguing*.

The former is something we tend to do when we are home alone. We grumble, moan, and find fault. We mutter under our breath. We whine and whinge about anything and everything that does not take our fancy. We carp because roses have thorns instead of being thankful that thorns have roses.

The man is a wise man, therefore, who heeds the word in Acts 6:1 as that should be a salutary warning to us that when griping and grousing starts we are walking on precariously thin ice.

The latter is a characteristic that more often than not happens when we are with others. It is vocal abuse, much of which is fluently spoken. It is open warfare on other people's character and ministry. It is making a song and dance about everything under the sun and doing it in such a way so as to stir up feelings of distrust and suspicion.

When we put the two of them together it causes verbal pollution of such magnitude that it takes a heavy toll on all those involved. The atmosphere is poisoned and lives are ruined because of acid rain comments.

Someone has said that the Lord created the world in six days, rested on the seventh and, on the eighth, started taking complaints.

- Do not allow yourself to have an argumentative spirit—it only divides.
- Do not specialise in causing friction—it only disrupts the family.
- Do not sow seeds of discontent—it only discredits the unimpeachable name of Jesus.

A certain man met his death in tragic circumstances. At his funeral, the minister waxed eloquent in his oratory. He praised the deceased for one thing after another. He went on, and on, and on. When the widow had just about had enough, she whispered to her son sitting beside her: 'Son, step up there and see if that is your father in that coffin!'

Another man, renowned for his constant complaining, was on the receiving end of a substantial sum of money. When he got his hands on it, he complained to his wife that it was not as much as he thought it should be. Within days, however, he bought a farm. He asked his wife what she thought they should name it. She told him: 'Why don't you call it Belly Acres!'

All right, we get the message, Paul! No need to shout, scream, or make a scene. Just shine!

Walk tall

We should be distinctively different from the nonChristian. There is no need to pontificate from a soapbox or stand and shout it from the rooftops as it will be glaringly obvious to all with eyes to see that we wear our Christianity on our shirt sleeves.

An Irishman was strolling through a graveyard reading the epitaphs on various headstones. One of them said: 'Here lies a lawyer and an honest man.' The man from the Emerald Isle reacted by blurting out: 'Faith and begoree, two men buried in the same grave!' We smile but there are times when we are like two men in one suit—schizophrenic saints—the one we are in profession and the one we are in practice.

To live a life that is *blameless* is to live with integrity so that no one can point an accusing finger. It is putting probity—trustworthiness—

back into everyday living. Another quality Paul expects to find in our lives is that of being *pure*. The thought here is of that which is unmixed and unadulterated. It is the picture of innocence, someone who is inexperienced in evil and untainted in motive. It is staying clean in a corrupt society. It is walking through the coal mine of this world without getting dirty. To be *without fault* is to be free of defect or blemish. The word that Paul used finds its origin in the sacrificial lambs that were destined for the altar. It is to be above and beyond reproach.

Among the souvenirs in the Mark Twain Memorial in Hartford, Connecticut are some autographed words written on white paper and neatly framed: 'Always do right. It will gratify some people and astonish the rest!'

A young Christian girl was out one evening on the town with her nonChristian friends. They were trying to entice her into some unsavoury places. She refused and headed back home. Before she went, they said: 'Are you scared of your dad? If you went in there for a bit of fun, would he hurt you?' The girl paused for a moment and then she said: 'No, he wouldn't. I'm afraid if I went in there I would hurt my father!'

The standards are high. They have to be. In a world of forty shades of grey, where anything goes, we should be men and women who stand out in a crowd. This is a lucid call to cheerful living in a world that secretes unhappiness. It is a clarion call to walk straight in a pagan society that is warped and crooked.

Men today are so twisted they could easily hide behind a corkscrew.

That is why we should be walking tall with our heads held high for Jesus. In a community riddled with so much that is foul and filthy, we ought to be shining as luminaries for the Lord. That is a fitting illustration of something that does what it has to do by being what it ought to be.

The famous novelist, Robert Louis Stevenson, recalls how one evening as a child he stood transfixed at his nursery window watching the lamplighter in the street. When his nanny asked the boy what he was doing, he replied: 'I'm watching the man knocking holes in the darkness.'

2:16a

Hold out!

We are to seize every opportunity afforded to us to share the word of life with others—*hold out (epechō) the word (logos) of life (zōē)*. In a world that is decadent, dark, and dead, it is the word of God alone that can bring about lasting change. Because it is known as the *word of life* it implies there is life in the word. And there is.

- We need to hold it fast—on the defensive.
- We need to hold it forth—on the offensive.

The phrase that Paul employs to describe this act is most vivid and graphic. It paints the picture of a host offering a refreshing chilled drink to an honoured guest at a banquet or celebration. That is what the gospel entails for it represents the gracious offer of Christ to those who do not know him.

What a challenge! There is the purpose that needs to be achieved—we cannot stop the world and jump off. We would be foolish to adopt the ostrich mentality and bury our heads in the sand and pretend it is not as bad as they say it is. We dare not risk becoming spiritual hermits living in isolation. We cannot opt out, or cop out. We are here. And because of what Jesus did, we owe it to him to implement it in our present environment.

Portia, in Shakespeare's *Merchant of Venice*, says:

How far that little candle throws its beam.
So shines a good deed in our naughty world.

2:16b-18

A joy in the there and then

Paul refers here to the day of Christ when he says: *in order that I may boast (kauchēma) on the day of Christ that I did not run (trechō) or labour (kopiaō) for nothing (kenos).* This is the same moment he spoke of previously in 1:6 as the day of accountability. Paul lived his life bearing in mind the upcoming judgment seat of Christ. He performed his daily round of service with eternity indelibly written on his heart and soul. He lived today in the light of tomorrow.

Today he was with them—tomorrow he may be with him. And he did not want to be ashamed or embarrassed. He longed that his life's work might redound to God's glory. As he looked back over many years he wanted to be able to do it with a sense of real satisfaction and pleasure. That brought joy.

Up in smoke

Such a laudable attitude finds its focus in sacrifice and service; strange bedfellows to produce joy, you may be tempted to think. Paul is simply walking down the same road that Jesus walked before him when he writes: *But even if I am being poured out like a drink offering (spendō) on the sacrifice (thysia) and service (leitourgia) coming from your faith (pistis), I am glad (chairō) and rejoice (synchairō) with all of you. So you too should be glad and rejoice with me.*

Paul sees himself as a drink offering—he has poured out his life and love on the altar for Jesus. And for them. As he emptied himself so God filled him to overflowing with a joy that was exorbitantly outrageous. He was a man saturated with the presence and power of a rejuvenating, reviving God.

In the sacrificial system, under the old covenant, the priest would take the animal sacrifices and spread them on the altar to be consumed by fire. Then they would take a drink offering—a liquid offering—and pour it on top of that searing hot flame. Inevitably the liquid would turn into steam and it would go up in a wisp of smoke.

Paul was more or less saying: I love people and I am here to serve people and to sacrifice for people so very much that, if necessary, I am willing for my life to just go up in steam to the Lord that I might be a blessing to other people.

It was said of the nineteenth-century Bishop of Liverpool, J C Ryle, that he woke each morning and thought of his bed as an altar, so dedicating himself as a living sacrifice to God at the outset of each new day.

When it comes to serving Jesus, it is always a matter of striking a balance. If we want to maintain a spiritual equilibrium, we will need to realise that God works in and we work out. Then and only then will we find as Warren Wiersbe says that 'life is not a series of disappointing ups and downs. Rather, it is a sequence of delightful ins and outs.'

Great minds think alike

The story is told of a repair man who crawled high up into the steeple of a church early one morning to investigate a problem with the ventilation system. To his chagrin he slipped and, as he began to fall, he grabbed the rope that was connected to the church bell. Needless to say, he woke up the whole town!

Sometimes life is like that! We find out that even ordinary experiences have repercussions far beyond what anyone could ever imagine. A small event can have massive consequences—I somehow recall that World War 1 began when the Archduke Franz Ferdinand, heir to the throne of Austria-Hungary, and his wife Sophie were assassinated. The death of two people set in motion the death of millions.

Similarly, a token act of kindness can have unpredictably beneficial consequences. Edward Kimball certainly had no idea that one of the boys in his Sunday School class, who had such difficulty understanding the gospel, would eventually shake two continents for God. Despite his obscure beginnings as a shoe salesman, D L Moody went on to become one of the world's greatest evangelists, and his legacy continues.

The same happened to the apostle Paul. He was on his first missionary journey in Acts 14 when he found himself in the Lycaonian cities of Lystra and Derbe. He and Barnabas were preaching their hearts out when the unthinkable happened. A miracle took place and within minutes the crowd were convinced that they had come from another planet—'the gods have come down to us in human form' (Acts 14:11).

Paul tried unsuccessfully to convince the people that they were human just like them. He even tore the shirt off his back in an attempt to reveal their plain vanilla humanity. It did not work! It was not long until rent a mob gathered from another town and began to stone the two preachers. Paul was dragged outside the city and left for dead. The next day they moved on to Derbe where a mighty work of grace took place in that they 'won a large number of disciples' (Acts 14:21).

It was in either Lystra or Derbe, amid all the mayhem and miracles, that Paul bumped into Timothy in the enquiry room. He listened to the young man's story. He heard about his parents. His mother, Eunice, was of Jewish origin. His father, whose name is unknown, was of Greek extraction, no doubt a pagan intellectual. It would appear that Timothy's childhood upbringing was more strongly influenced by his father because he was not circumcised until he was a young adult.

At the same time, it is obvious that Timothy's maternal grandmother, Lois, played a leading role in his life. Together, with his mother, they sought to give him a good grounding in the things of the Lord (*cf.* 2 Timothy 1:5, 3:14, 15). Both of them were godly ladies. There must have been something beautiful and attractive about their joint witness in the home. So much so that when Paul arrived on the scene, young Timothy was quick to respond to the good news of Jesus. He was hand-picked fruit, ripe and ready to be plucked for the Lord.

We have no way of knowing how long Paul spent counselling Timothy on that memorable day, it may have been 25 or 30 minutes or more. Who, in their wildest dreams, could have anticipated the outcome of that conversation? Who ever would have thought then that a short time later Paul would return to this same area on his second missionary journey and invite Timothy to join him?

Paul was impressed by his teachable spirit and love for God's truth. He saw sterling qualities in Timothy that eclipsed his youthful countenance. Fantastic! Read all about it in Acts 16:1-3. This heralded the start of a lifelong friendship when Timothy proved to be worth more than his weight in gold.

- They laughed together.
- They cried together.
- They preached together.
- They travelled together.

There was nothing forced or stilted about their relationship, it just flowed naturally. There was instantaneous rapport. It was all so easy-looking and enormously rewarding. In fact, it was such a high profile partnership that Timothy is mentioned twenty-four times in Paul's letters and is identified with Paul in the writing of five epistles.

After many years of fruitful service together, when the older man was promoted to glory, his successor was Timothy (*cf.* 2 Timothy 4:1-11). He had been groomed for such a role and was ready to fill it when occasion deemed it was right. That was wise planning on Paul's part and a worthwhile investment of his expertise in the life of another individual— classic textbook material on mentoring in ministry. It works!

2:19

You're the man to go

These words are a window into the heart and mind of Paul. He is extremely well-organised and seems to have no hangups about delegating responsibility. He is fairly relaxed when it comes to telling other people what to do and where to go. It is clear from his epistle that he is happy to block out a few days in another man's diary so that he can receive an up-to-the-minute report on life in Philippi.

We read: *I hope (elpizō) in the Lord Jesus to send Timothy to you soon (tacheōs), that I also may be cheered (eupsycheō) when I receive news (ginōskō) about you.*

2:20

When D+J=P+T

So far as Paul is concerned, the obvious candidate for the job was Timothy. He flatly confesses that he has *no one (oudeis) else like (isopsychos) him.* Talk about great minds thinking alike! These guys were on the same wavelength. They were batting from the same crease. A mathematician would say that their triangles were congruent.

Charles Swindoll makes the point that '... they thought alike. Their perspectives were in line with each other. Timothy would interpret situations much like Paul, had the latter been there. When the older man sent the younger on a fact finding mission he could rely on the report as being similar to one he himself would have brought back.'

There was a oneness of spirit between them. I imagine it was not unlike the closeness David enjoyed with Jonathan (*cf.* 1 Samuel 18:1, 20:17). There was a unique and unusual depth in their understanding of each other, neither would have to speak because the one knew what the other was thinking.

A caring heart

Paul cannot speak highly enough of young Timothy. He is fulsome in his praise. He reminds them that Timothy *takes a genuine (gnēsiōs) interest (merimnaō) in [their] welfare.* He loves people. He cares for people. He is concerned about the needs of others. He wants to do all he can to alleviate their suffering—this guy has a big heart for people—full stop.

'There are no uninteresting things, there are only uninterested people.' (G K Chesterton)

Many years ago Dwight Morrow told a group of friends that he felt Calvin Coolidge had a real chance of becoming President of the USA. To a man they disagreed saying that Mr Coolidge was boringly quiet, lacking colour and charisma. One member of the caucus reckoned people just 'would not like him.'

At that point in the proceedings, Dwight Morrow's daughter Ann spoke up: 'Well, you may not like him, but I do!' Then the six-year-old girl held up a bandaged finger and said: 'He was the only one who asked me about my sore finger!' Her father nodded, and said: 'Gentlemen, there is your answer.'

Paul had no reservations lurking in the back of his mind about his choice of personal envoy. He knew Timothy could handle the people well without adding to the tension they were experiencing. Old man Paul can rest easy because young man Timothy would sooner be part of the answer, rather than part of the problem.

2:21

One in a million

Can you imagine? There were tens of hundreds of Christians in Rome, yet not one was available to make this short mission trip across to Philippi. Not one! Reason: they were too busy doing their own thing to worry about anyone else. Paul makes the observation that *everyone looks out for his own interests, not those of Jesus Christ.*

That same mindset is reflected in a few prayers I stumbled across in recent days. There is the prayer of a certain father: 'Lord, bless me and my wife, my son John and his wife, us four and no more!' Then there is the prayer of a childless couple: 'Lord, bless us two, and that will do!' To round it off, there is the prayer of a bachelor: 'Lord, bless only me, that's as far as I can see!'

They were immersed in themselves and could not see any further than their own noses. If it was not in their backyard they showed an appalling dearth of interest. They were totally wrapped up in their own affairs as spiritual Sinn Feiners—meaning: 'we ourselves'.

So much for their spirituality. Or lack! It says a lot about their exiguity of consecration and commitment to the body of Christ. They needed to sort themselves out when it came to assessing priorities.

In a very real sense, all of us live either in Philippians 1:21 or Philippians 2:21.

2:22

Unsung hero

Paul has a wonderful way with words as he quietly reassures the church as to Timothy's suitability for the job in hand. It is the power of positive thinking as he says: *But you know that Timothy has proved (dokimē) himself, because as a son (teknon) with his father (patēr) he has served (douleuō) with me in the work of the gospel (euangelion).*

In other words, he has served his apprenticeship well. It was a steep learning curve but he has come through every test with flying colours. Timothy is a man of calibre. Quality personified. He has character and mettle. Paul was not the only one who spoke in such glowing language—remember the statement recorded by the leaders of his local church: 'the brothers at Lystra and Iconium spoke well of him' (Acts 16:2).

The apostle gave him lots of practical experience in various situations so that he would develop an all-round ministry. His was on the job, in-house training and it proved to be more than satisfactory. Timothy probably did not realise it at the time but it was a privilege for him to learn firsthand from the greatest exponent in the early church on how-to and how-not-to do it.

2:23, 24

Future planning

I hope, therefore, to send him as soon as I see how things go with me. And I am confident (peithō) in the Lord that I myself will come soon. It is fairly obvious at this point that Paul has no idea how things will pan out in his own life. The court had not yet given its verdict—he did not know whether he was coming or going, whether he would be executed or released. It was all up in the air, as we often say.

By the same token, Paul is not in the least taken aback. He is not immersed in morbid self-pity nor is he languishing in the depths of despair. He looks forward to the unfolding of God's purpose in his life and, whatever that might entail, he is happy to go along with it.

2:25-28

Enter Epaphroditus

There is a subtle difference in the way Paul deals with Timothy and Epaphroditus *(Epaphroditos)*. Because of the exceptional relationship they enjoyed, Paul wrote of who Timothy was. But when he mentions this second gentleman—Epaphroditus—he puts his finger on what he did. (I wonder if the locals called him Pappy for short?)

- Timothy is a marvellous example of service, and
- Epaphroditus is a superb model of suffering.

He was no Johnny-come-lately on the church scene. On the contrary, he was a highly respected and well-known member of the Christian community in Philippi. He was specially commissioned by them to take a monetary gift to Paul and to stay with him as long as possible during his confinement in Rome. He was a man whom they could implicitly trust with such an important assignment.

After a relatively short time in Rome, Epaphroditus developed a serious life-threatening illness. He almost died. A man got up in a prayer meeting and shared: 'My wife's mother is at death's door. I want you to pray that God will pull her through!'

I do not know what happened to the mother-in-law but I do know what happened to Epaphroditus. Eventually he made a complete recovery. In between times, however, word filtered back to the church via the bush telegraph and, understandably, they were perplexed and perturbed about his rumoured condition. To make matters worse, he was worrying about them worrying about him.

Paul spells it out when he writes: *But I think it is necessary (anakaios) to send back to you Epaphroditus ... For he longs (epipotheō) for all of you and is distressed (adēmoneō) because you heard he was ill (astheneō). Indeed he was ill, and almost (paraplēsios) died (thanatos). But God had mercy (eleeō) on him, and not on him only but also on me, to spare me sorrow (lypē) upon sorrow. Therefore I am all the more eager (spoudaiōs) to send him, so that when you see him again you may be glad and I may have less anxiety (alypos).*

When the dust finally settled, Paul felt it prudent to send Epaphroditus back home so that the folks there would see for themselves how miraculously he had been restored to health. Paul was at pains to point out, in the course of his comments, that Epaphroditus was a tremendous blessing to him and he was standing by him with unswerving loyalty.

There may have been some gossip and criticism among the church members about him returning as a quitter, or some (with the benefit of hindsight) may have questioned his being the best choice in the first place. Paul quickly extinguished the smouldering embers of idle talk and damaging chitchat.

Always innovative and so as to kill two birds with one stone, Paul sent this letter back with him. That was how the church at Philippi received the epistle to the Philippians.

Meet Mr Charming

Yes, believe it or not, that is what his name means. He lived up to his name. I think if we met him downtown we would not be disappointed for he was a lovely man. A nice guy. His name is probably linked to Aphrodite, the pagan goddess of love, beauty, and gambling. Because of that, in the casinos, men would often cry out 'Epaphroditus' as they threw the dice on the table, hoping to be favoured by her.

'Apart from these few verses he would be an unknown, but in many respects, that fits him anyway. He was just a layman in the church at Philippi who held no office, wrote no books, gave no sermons, led no great enterprises for God. He was a messenger boy for the gospel, a servant for his Lord. No task was too menial for him to do. No assignment was too little for him to accept. No risk was too great for him to take. He would have been comfortable with a towel and basin.' (David Jeremiah)

Jack-of-all-trades

Paul clearly thought the sun rose and set on Epaphroditus. He counted him and valued him as a buddy, an extremely good friend and colleague. He was beau idéal. He described him as:

- *My brother (adelphos)*—they were bound by a common love because they were united as brothers in the same spiritual family. There was a warmth in their Christian experience. This is further elaborated on by Paul when we see his immense relief that his life was spared (*cf.* 2:27).
- *Fellow worker (synergos)*—they were both involved in the service of the Lord and were keen to see the gospel triumph in the hearts of men and women, boys and girls. He had an entrepreneurial spirit like Paul as they shared together in the ministry of the word of God.

- *Fellow soldier (systratiōtēs)*—it is never enough to be just a worker in the ministry, one must also learn as he did to be a warrior. Facing danger has an unusual way of bonding lives as men learn to depend on each other. There were many open doors but there were also many adversaries. It was a battle.

Mr E and the Parabolani

Never heard of them? Too good to miss! We read in 2:30 that Epaphroditus *[risked] his life* in order to minister effectively into the situation that Paul found himself in. It has the idea of someone hazarding their life for another. Such a person would gamble against the odds. The stakes might be high but they were willing to take the risk. They often visited prisoners and ministered to the sick and terminally ill, especially those with dangerous communicable diseases whom no one else would help or even go near with a disinfected bargepole.

If there was a slim chance of success they would put their money where their mouth was—the betting man's way of looking at life. Those people became known as the Parabolani or the Riskers. Our friend Epaphroditus, along with the likes of Aquila and Priscilla (*cf.* Romans 16:3, 4), were fully paid-up members of this four hundred club.

2:29, 30

Local hero

Paul encourages the church to *welcome (prosdechomai) him in the Lord with great joy, and honour (entimos) men like him, because he almost died for the work of Christ, risking (paraboleuomai) his life to make up for the help (leitourgia) you could not give me.* He deserves a hero's welcome when he gets back home. It should be an occasion for throwing a party in his honour, an excuse for a celebration. Deservedly so.

Men willing to do what Epaphroditus did are few and far between. These are men who dice with death and do not stop to ask questions. They flirt openly with all kinds of risk but they do it from a profound sense of loyalty to their friends and a consummate love for their Lord. These men, says Paul, are thin on the ground. We thank God for them!

The story is told of two inseparable friends who enlisted together, trained together, were shipped overseas together, and fought side by side in the trenches during World War 1. During an attack, one of the duo was critically wounded in a field filled with barbed wire obstacles and, because of that, was unable to crawl back to his foxhole. The entire area was under enemy crossfire and it was suicidal to try to reach him.

Nevertheless, undaunted, his friend decided to give it a go. Before he could get out of his own trench, his sergeant yanked him back and told him: 'You're mad. It's far too late. You can't do him any good and you'll only end up getting yourself killed.' A few minutes later the officer turned his back and instantly his mate was gone after his friend.

Shortly afterwards, he staggered back, mortally wounded, with his friend now dead in his arms. The sergeant was both angry and deeply moved. 'What a waste,' he blurted out. 'He's dead and you're dying. It just wasn't worth it.' With almost his last breath, the dying soldier retorted: 'O yes it was, for when I got to him, the only thing he said was, "I knew you would come, Jim".' The lesson is that Jim was there for his friend, when it cost!

When we look at the three of them—Paul, Timothy, and Epaphroditus—they are as different as day and night. Forget about Paul for a moment. Here were two very ordinary blokes, two special friends of Paul, two companions who lived in the shadow of the great man, two men from nowhere who were going somewhere.

One of them, Timothy, we hear and read a lot about; the other, Epaphroditus, appears and before we get our tongue around the pronunciation of his name, he has gone. He is only mentioned twice in Paul's letters.

Take Timothy and Epaphroditus, they were:

- ready to be sent anywhere,
- ready to serve anyone, and
- ready to sacrifice anything.

Add Paul to the equation and all three are a formidable trio of great minds thinking alike!

3

No thrill like knowing Jesus

3:1

Playing with words

I heard of a country preacher who came to the Sunday morning breakfast table with a laceration on his cheek. His wife asked him what happened. He told her that he was concentrating on his sermon while shaving and had cut himself. With a straight face, she said to him: 'Well, darling, maybe you should concentrate on your shaving and cut your sermon!'

Heard the latest definition of an optimist? An optimist is a person who believes the preacher is almost finished when he says 'finally'.

See the opening word in verse one. Yes, correctly sussed, it is that word: *finally*.

An interesting statistic is that in the first two chapters there is a total of 60 verses. The aggregate in the final two chapters is 44, yet Paul says *finally (loipos)*. He cannot be serious! And to further confuse the issue, he is only starting the second half of his epistle according to the chapter divisions. Makes you think!

So what does Paul mean when he says *finally*? It is almost like a change of gear as he moves into overdrive. He keeps on going and he has no intention of applying the brake just yet. He has not used the word in a conclusive sense for he could have said: 'as for the rest …'

Be joyful

If they failed to get the message first time, Paul was determined they would get it this time. Hence his comment: *rejoice (chairō) in the Lord.* This is the underlying theme of his letter and he wants to underscore the importance of them being a people whose life is categorised as joyful. Vital. Pivotal.

Happiness depends on happenings but, even when things go pear-shaped, we can still experience joy. The joy of the Lord is such that circumstances cannot change it. It is immune to the highs and lows of everyday life. It is not influenced by the emotional seesaw we sometimes are sitting on.

Our circumstances may be less than conducive to a life of joy, our present situation may cause us considerable concern and be a source of nagging worry to our minds, the forecast may sound menacingly ominous and, in such moments, we do not feel like jumping for joy.

But we can. This joy is not artificial. It is not a thin veneer of superficial praise smiles. It has nothing to do with grinning from ear to ear like a Cheshire cat. Joy, like laughter, is a tranquiliser with no side effects. This joy is fixed and rooted in Jesus Christ for he is the source of true joy, the force of real joy, and he sets the course for all joy.

We may not be able to rejoice in our circumstances. And that is fine. But it does not matter what life throws at us, we can still rejoice in the Lord (*cf.* Habakkuk 3:17, 18). It is contagious. And unexplainable. Even outrageous.

'Joy is the feeling of grinning inside.' (Melba Cosgrove)

The apostle is really setting the tone for the rest of the chapter. Principally, they were not to rejoice in who they were and what they achieved, but they were to rejoice in Jesus Christ and all that he accomplished. That is why Paul makes no apology for retracing his steps and going back over old ground: *It is no trouble (oknēros) for me to write (graphō) the same things to you again, and it is a safeguard (asphalēs) for you.*

Paul believes, like every competent educator, that repetition is the mother of all learning—say something often enough and people will eventually get the message. It sinks in, given time. It is good pedagogy.

A bit like the black preacher who said: *'I preach very simply. First, I tell them what I'm going to tell them. Then I tell them. Then I tell them what I just told them!'*

Not like the wife who burst into tears when she told her husband: 'I can't remember the last time you told me you loved me.' The husband responded: 'I told you forty-seven years ago when we got married that I loved you and, if I ever change my mind, don't worry, I'll be sure to let you know!'

Well, Paul never grew tired or weary of telling these dear people to enjoy the sumptuous blessings God gave to them in the Lord Jesus. So far as Paul is concerned, joy should be near the top of the list.

3:2

Alarm bells ringing

Paul's language is less than complimentary when he sees what is happening on the ground in Philippi. There is a hint of realistic sarcasm in the tone of his voice as he labels false teachers for what they really are. Explosive material. Hence the terse *watch out.*

They should be on red alert as the enemy was alive and well in their community. It was a real challenge to them to be constantly on guard, looking over their shoulder, as well as looking ahead. They have been warned. Pray, by all means, but do not close your eyes.

The tendency is for us to become so comfortable, complacent, and cushioned in our Christianity that, before we know it, carelessness has swept like an unassailable tidal wave into our lives. We are maybe not as vigilant as we ought to be or as conscious of the enemy's tactics as we should be. Paul says, beware!

A triple whammy

This is incredibly strong language. Paul is bold and blunt as he brands them with a triple warning: *... dogs ... men who do evil ... mutilators of the flesh.* Boom! Boom! Boom! Note that Paul is not referring to three different groups of people, he is describing the same group in three different ways. These are Judaisers whose religion is a mixture of law and grace.

The advertising moguls tell us that a dog is a man's best friend. Maybe. Maybe not. When Paul refers to them as *dogs (kyon),* he does not have in mind the family pet that we pamper and play with. It is not the pampered Pedigree Chum kind of dog with a Cruft's medal hanging around its neck. He is talking about people. Real people. In his day, the orthodox Jew would call a Gentile a 'dog' (*cf.* Matthew 15:26)—here the shoe is on the other foot when Paul refers to them as *dogs.* Pariah dogs.

They are Christians of the canine variety.

Paul is not in the business of slinging mud at people. Nor is he into calling names. He is, however, comparing these false teachers to dirty, disease-carrying scavengers who are potentially dangerous. They snap at your heels. They bark out their erroneous doctrine and pose a minatory threat to anyone who is unsuspecting. Troublemakers.

Synthetic saints

These guys are *men who do evil (kakos).* Jesus referred to them as 'wolves in sheep's clothing' (Matthew 7:15). They are a certain breed of pernicious individuals who wriggle and worm their way into a congregation and teach that a sinner is saved by faith plus good works. Legalists. It has been said of them that 'their message is full of exhortations to do more, to work harder, to witness longer, to pray with greater intensity, because enough is never enough.'

Yes, they sing all the new worship songs and use the latest technology. They are the tee shirt and blue denim brigade. The smooth talker. The financially secure. The smart and smarmy young man or woman with an effervescent personality. The church needs to beware of them as they peddle their wares on unsuspecting saints. Do not be fooled!

A cut around

An interesting turn of phrase is applied when Paul calls them *mutilators (katatomē) of the flesh.* The word 'mutilation' refers to the cutting of circumcision. In other words, when these false teachers required the young believers to be circumcised in order to be saved, they were guilty of mutilating the flesh of these brethren. Their confidence was in the flesh.

The fact of the matter is that the true Christian has experienced a spiritual circumcision in Christ, therefore, he does not need any fleshly operation.

These men invite you to come to Christ with the Bible in one hand and a sharp surgical knife in the other.

It is easy to understand why Paul came down so hard on these men, he came down on them with a ton of bricks. They posed a very real threat to the people of God in the first century. He knew if he gave them an inch, they would take more than the customary mile. Do not be hoodwinked! Do not be caught napping! Do not be conned! They are no more than a bunch of spiritual crooks, guilty of spiritual piracy.

Two millennia later

The problem is as real in the third millennium as it was in the early days of the primitive church. The straight-up, no beating about the bush challenge from Paul is just as relevant too.

S. Lewis Johnson skilfully unmasks the villain of the piece in a remarkable exposé when he concludes that '... one of the most serious problems facing the orthodox Christian church today is the problem of legalism. One of the most serious problems facing the church in Paul's day was the problem of legalism. In every day it is the same.

'Legalism wrenches the joy of the Lord from the Christian believer, and with the joy of the Lord goes his power for vital worship and vibrant witness. Nothing is left but cramped, sombre, dull, and listless profession. The truth is betrayed, and the glorious name of the Lord becomes a synonym for a gloomy killjoy. The Christian under the law is a miserable parody of the real thing.'

'Legalism has no pity on people. It makes my opinion your burden, your boundary, and your obligation.' (Max Lucado)

3:3, 4

Worship as God intended

Paul communicates the simple truth to his friends in Philippi when he shows the remarkable difference between them and the false teachers in a classic 'them and us' scenario. They glory in who and what they are—we glory in the person and work of Jesus Christ.

Says Paul: *we are the circumcision (peritomē).* Daring statement. Indeed. Our salvation is not something outward, it is a deep inner work of the Holy Spirit in the life of the child of God. It is not found in some ancient religious ritual or sacerdotal ceremony, it lies exclusively in the finished work of Christ on Calvary. It is not for the body, it is a matter for the heart. We are a covenant people. How do we show it?

A heart response

Paul reminds us that we are those *who worship (latreuō) by the Spirit of God.* True spiritual worship—authentic, biblical, God-orientated worship—is conducted in the human heart in the power of the Holy Spirit. This finds an echo in the sentiments of Jesus Christ recorded in John 4:24, and is also indicative of the desire expressed by David in Psalm 24:4.

It is when we are occupied with him and taken in with him, that he becomes central in our love and devotion—this can only happen when the Spirit is ruling and reigning within us. 'The essence of worship is living a life of obedient service to God,' notes John MacArthur.

Glory to God

Paul takes his argument a step further when he describes us as those *who glory (kauchaomai) in Christ Jesus*. That means the Christian finds his joy in Jesus. He becomes number one in our lives for he is Lord of all. We exult in the exalted one.

Martin Luther was surprised one day when his wife Katy went upstairs and changed into black clothing. *'What's wrong, dear?'* the great reformer asked her. She replied: *'By the look of you, I thought that God had died an hour ago.'*

In ourselves we have absolutely nothing to commend us. Left to go our own way we would be hopelessly lost, but when the heart is captivated by him, then all the praise is ascribed to him. He gets all the glory. Rightly so.

The great refusal

Paul declares we *put no confidence (peithō) in the flesh (sarx)*. There is nothing we can do in our old nature to win the Father's smile of approval. There is no good in any one of us that merits a place in heaven. The old man has nothing going for it, it wars against the spiritual new nature. I cannot do it. He can.

Our dependence is solely upon him for he is the rock on which we stand. Enormous relief. God's grace has once again come to our aid and rescue. And in the process he gets every bit of the glory. All the credit goes to him, as certainly it should (*cf.* Galatians 6:14).

I appreciate the way Matt Redman develops this truth:

Jesus Christ,
I think upon your sacrifice;
You became nothing,
Poured out to death.
Many times I've wondered
At your gift of life,
And I'm in that place once again,
I'm in that place once again.

And once again I look upon
The cross where you died,
I'm humbled by your mercy
And I'm broken inside.
Once again I thank you,
Once again I pour out my life.

Now you are exalted
To the highest place,
King of the heavens,
Where one day I'll bow.
But for now
I marvel at this saving grace,
And I'm full of praise once again,
I'm full of praise once again.

Charles Swindoll feels that when Paul was writing such words 'he must have experienced a flashback to the way he was for so many years— in fact, all of his adult life. Before his conversion, he was the personification of a proud Pharisee. Nobody's trophy case was larger. Had they given an award for high achievement in the field of religion, Paul would have won top honours in his nation year after year. His wall could have been covered with plaques, diplomas, framed letters from influential individuals, and numerous artefacts—all impressive.'

Paul gave them the once-over, then looked at himself in his former days and, in all honesty, there was no match. They were in a different league to him—he was in the upper echelons of the premier league, they were languishing in the lower divisions. They would have an awful lot of ground to make up if they were going to catch up with Paul. A virtual impossibility.

He was the king of his own castle. They were left standing outside, shivering in the cold, as also-rans. Yesterday's men. Therein lies the significance behind Paul's inspired reasoning when he says: *If anyone else thinks (dokeō) he has reasons to put confidence in the flesh, I have more.* Paul has the credentials to prove it. He has the black and white record to back up all that he says about himself. He was as straight as a gun barrel.

Paul was a high flyer. He has the CV of a high achiever.

3:5, 6

Personal portfolio

Paul gives us his résumé in these verses by going back to his roots before his conversion, before God grabbed him by the ears and remade everything about him—an autobiographical sketch where Paul traces his heritage and records his many outstanding achievements. He outstripped his contemporaries, he eclipsed all other lights. He was a giant among pygmies. In comparison to him, they suffer from the grasshopper complex.

Paul testifies that he was *circumcised (peritomē) on the eighth (oktaēmeros) day, of the people (genos) of Israel (Israēl), of the tribe (phylē) of Benjamin (Beniamin), a Hebrew (Hebraios) of Hebrews; in regard to the law (nomos), a Pharisee (Pharisaios); as for zeal (zēlos), persecuting (diōkō) the church (ekklēsia); as for legalistic (nomos) righteousness (dikaiosynē), faultless (amemptos).*

What a pedigree. Wow! Crème de la crème.

W B on Paul

William Barclay in his book, *The Mind of St Paul*, explains the thinking behind each of these seven assets listed by Paul. He writes: 'If ever there was a Jew who was steeped in Judaism, that Jew was Paul. Let us ... look again at the claims he had to be the Jew par excellence.

'He was *circumcised on the eighth day*—that is to say, he bore in his body the badge and the mark that he was one of the chosen people, marked out by God as his own. He was of *the people of Israel*—that is to say, he was a member of the nation who stood in a covenant relationship with God, a relationship in which no other people stood.

'He was *of the tribe of Benjamin*—this is a claim which Paul reiterates in Romans 11:1. What is the point of this claim? The tribe of Benjamin had a unique place in the history of Israel. It was from Benjamin that the first king of Israel had come, for Saul was a Benjamite … Benjamin was the only one of the patriarchs who had actually been born in the land of promise. When Israel went into battle, it was this tribe which held the post of honour. The battle cry of Israel was, "After thee, O Benjamin".

'In lineage, Paul was not only an Israelite, he was of the aristocracy of Israel for he was *a Hebrew of Hebrews*—that is to say, Paul was not one of those Jews of the Dispersion who, in a foreign land, forgot their own tongue; he was a Jew who still remembered and knew the language of his fathers.

'He was *a Pharisee*—that is to say, he was not only a devout Jew, he was more, he was one of "The Separated Ones" who had foresworn all normal activities in order to dedicate their life to the keeping of the law, and he had kept it with such meticulous care that in the keeping of it he was blameless.

'Paul knew Judaism at its best and at its highest; he knew it from the inside; he had gone through all the experiences, both of height and of depth, that it could bring to any man.'

God on Paul

An amazing man. Exemplary. Full of earnest endeavour. And grand qualifications. He could boast in his ancestry and his orthodoxy. What he did backed up all he believed. There was no contradiction between his belief system and his behaviour. He talked the talk. He walked the walk. He was a paragon of virtue. No man could justifiably point an accusing finger at him.

When it came to morality, Paul was as clean as a hounds tooth. If being good, decent, and upright could transport a man to heaven, Paul would have ridden first class.

This guy had it made! He had it all! It just had not been set apart for God's use. The radical difference came about when he met Jesus on the Damascus road. There and then he quickly discovered that all of the achievements he tucked under his belt meant nothing in the light of the righteousness of Christ.

He had enough religion to take him to church but he did not have enough righteousness to take him to heaven. All that he attained and worked hard for faded into oblivion when weighed in the scales of divine justice. Staggering. Mr Spurgeon said that 'morality can keep a man out of jail, but only Jesus can keep a man out of hell.'

By the world's tape measure, Paul's success was phenomenal. By God's standard, it was piffling and paltry.

Standing before Jesus Christ, blinded by a heavenly light, Paul was humbled for the first time in his life. He realised he had nothing to offer as he was stripped of all his assets. He knew deep down that he was a nobody. Only a cipher.

It only took a split second in the awesome presence of the Lord of glory for Paul to realise that, up to this point, he had spent his entire life on the wrong road, travelling towards the wrong destination, for all the wrong reasons. Not the cleverest thing in the world!

It was the *nothing in my hands I bring, simply to thy cross I cling* time for Saul of Tarsus. Make up your mind time. His hour of decision. Thank God, he did not flinch from making the wise choice.

When Jesus Christ invaded the life of this religious fanatic, he performed a creative act. A miracle of metamorphosis. An inside-out transformation. Just as a caterpillar's whole body dissolves in the cocoon and is restructured into a stunningly beautiful butterfly, so our entire being melts away into a brand new life in Jesus Christ—a new creation (*cf.* 2 Corinthians 5:17).

When George Truett was pastor of First Baptist Church in Dallas, Texas a sceptic came up to him after a Sunday service. He remonstrated with him and this is what he said: 'Dr Truett, I want you to tell me the truth. Is Jesus Christ real to you?' The preacher man looked at him with that square jaw and said: 'Sir, Jesus is more real to me than the air that I breathe and the skin on my flesh.'

That was Paul. He was reconciled and given a transfusion of joy. He was unconditionally forgiven and unreservedly accepted into the global family of God. He had religion, and lots of it—now he has reality. That is why he encourages them to *rejoice in the Lord.*

3:7

Taking a spiritual inventory

The story is told of the toddler who fell out of bed. When he did, his mum asked him what happened. Little Johnny told her: *'I stayed too near where I got in!'*

You smile. I smile. But we did not land on the hard floor! Nevertheless, that is how it is with many of the Lord's people today—they stay too near where they get in. That could never be said of the apostle Paul. He was always on the move, always crossing new frontiers for the gospel, always stepping out where man had never been before with the story of redemption. But it was not always like that.

He and David share one common trait—both can say that 'the boundary lines have fallen for me in pleasant places; surely I have a delightful inheritance' (Psalm 16:6). He had a heritage to be proud of. He was an intellectual genius. Savvy. He successfully climbed the social ladder. His was the name dropped by everybody who was anybody. He made it to the top. And stayed there. Until …

From a human point of view, Paul was born with a silver spoon in his mouth. Then, out of the blue, something happened that was to radically modify the course of his life. He would never be the same again.

I was there when it happened

He met Jesus. Miraculous. Life-changing. He was pirouetted around on the expressway of life to face a new direction. He was turned inside out and given a new outlook and perspective on life. God stopped him in the leafy suburbs of Damascus and called a halt to his maddening pace. He was going nowhere fast. And when the Saviour laid hold of him, his whole life was dramatically revamped. Needless to say, this was when Paul really started to live.

Sensational stuff—a front page story to give the local press a field day. Imagine the bold headlines emblazoned across the tabloids. The *Daily Whatever-you-want-to-call-it* would have no hesitation capitalising on such a scoop. A fortune is in the making. The cash registers ring non-stop. This is the kind of story that sells newspapers.

There's more to life than ...

Paul has a new frame of reference for everything in his life has changed as a result of his spiritual mutation. He quickly discovered that there is more to life than ... all he had before. He penned it like this: *But whatever was to my profit (kerdos) I now consider (hēgeomai) loss (zēmia) for the sake of Christ.*

His values are reversed. They are up-ended. These are not the words of a modest man—these are the words of a man transformed by Jesus Christ. It seems as if Paul is sitting down at his sturdy mahogany desk with the book of his life open before him. He tots up the figures. He looks at the credit and debit entries. When he finishes, he produces a profit and loss account.

Paul is taking stock of his position. He is in review mode. He is making a spiritual inventory so that he can accurately assess where he is at. And when he looks at the computer printout, it is fairly obvious what has happened—the whole picture has shifted because of one major transaction.

In one column, there was all of this: his impeccable pedigree, his outstanding past, his fantastic achievements, his personal portfolio, his impressive array of qualifications—all gains—for Paul was no nincompoop.

See what has taken place.

Every single entry—all his trophies, gold medals, and blue ribbons—have moved from the asset column to the liability column. He has nothing. Zilch. That is where four plus three equals a minus. The mathematics of joy.

At the same time, in the other column, only one standalone entry is recorded—his never-to-be-forgotten conversion to Jesus Christ. He has everything.

When gain is loss and loss is gain

When Paul speaks of his deficit total he uses the word *loss*—a word only found in two other places in the New Testament. Ironically, it is mentioned in Acts 27:10, 21 where it describes the loss and damage suffered by the ship on which Paul was taken as a prisoner to Rome. This provides us with a real life illustration of how gain can turn to loss.

The Italy-bound ship had cargo aboard which was meant to bring considerable profit to its owner. If the crew had not thrown it over the side, all passengers on board were potential casualties. The cargo was jettisoned, the ship ran aground breaking its back, but the passengers and crew were all saved (*cf.* Acts 27:38-41).

Everything intended for gain became loss so that the lives of men and women might be saved. Similarly, with the apostle Paul, all the cargo of his past life was thrown overboard so that he might gain his own spiritual life in Jesus Christ.

Jim Eliot, one of five missionaries to the Auca Indians of Ecuador martyred on 8 January 1956, hit the nail on the head when he scripted in his 1949 journal: *He is no fool who gives what he cannot keep to gain what he cannot lose.*

3:8, 9

Time marches on

Three decades have come and gone. Has Paul? Let him speak for himself: *What is more, I consider everything a loss compared to the surpassing greatness (hyperechō) of knowing (gnōsis) Christ Jesus my Lord, for whose sake I have lost all things. I consider them rubbish (skybalon), that I may gain (kerdainō) Christ and be found (heuriskō) in him, not having a righteousness of my own that comes from the law, but that which is through faith in Christ—the righteousness that comes from God and is by faith.*

The passing of time has not diminished his zeal for the Lord nor has it dampened his enthusiasm in serving the greatest Master of all. A lot of water has gone under the bridge in thirty years but Paul still aims high in his rigorous quest for intimacy in his knowledge of Christ.

He says this after he has tried it and found it really works. Here is the voice of experience. He has no doubts in his mind. There is not even a tinge of disappointment. At the second count, he reckons there is nothing in this world that can be compared with the heart's pursuit of God. There is a thrill in knowing Jesus. It gives a tingle that nothing else can. A buzz. Getting to know God better has to be seen as the ultimate adventure.

It involves the mind of the Christian for we apply ourselves to a serious study of the word of God. As we become better acquainted with him in the pages of Scripture, so we familiarise ourselves with the imposing doctrines of grace and glory. We become avid readers of the sacred page and keen listeners to the preached word.

It also goes a few inches lower captivating the affections of the heart. When our minds are stirred and our hearts are warmed, it all becomes so meaningful, up-close, and personal when we can jubilantly exclaim with Thomas: 'My Lord and my God!' (John 20:28).

Fit for the tip

When Paul analyses his present position in Christ he is overwhelmed. He is almost lost for words as he knows he is immeasurably better off. He has a copious richness in his life that money cannot buy. His knowledge of the living God is worth more than acres of diamonds.

Everything else, says Paul, is worthless. Rubbish fit for a refuse tip. His past and all the glories associated with it are as good as trash and ideal consumption for dogs and vermin. In reality, they are of no more value than leftovers. Garbage. Debris. Junk. Ideal stuff for an incinerator.

He lost but he's not a loser

Paul lost his reputation and his religion but he gained far more than he lost. He is not a loser in either the short term or the long term. God never short-changes his people. Paul is now *found in him* and he could not be in a better place. There is no safer place on planet earth.

Because of his relationship with the Lord he has also been made righteous. The righteousness of Jesus Christ has been imparted and imputed to him. This is not the works righteousness we read of in verse 6 but the faith righteousness spoken of in verse 9. The former depends on the sinner—the latter depends on the Saviour. What happened was this: sin was transferred *from* his account and righteousness transferred *to* his account. That is God's system of bookkeeping.

Charles Swindoll says: 'At that epochal moment, divine righteousness was credited to his empty account and he saw himself clothed in the imputed righteousness of Christ. That changed everything within him and about him.'

Try to imagine the blinding, searing, white fire at the core of a new star blazing in the heavens. Now ... what if you could take that searing radiance and just slip it over your shoulders like a robe? That just begins to describe what it means to have the righteousness of Jesus—the perfect, sinless, spotless Lamb of God—covering all of your life.

Charitie L. Bancroft (1841-92) was on the same track when she wrote:

Behold him there! The risen Lamb!
My perfect, spotless Righteousness.

In another man's shoes

No wonder Paul has a joy that is blissfully outrageous. No more is he wrapped up in the trinkets and baubles of religion. No longer is he interested in all the holy hardware with its trimmings and trappings. For too many years he knew he was engrossed in a cheap, hand down religion, now he has the real McCoy. He has found to his immense personal pleasure that Christianity is Christ and, because of that, he can gleefully sing with the hymnwriter: *He is my everything, he is my all.*

The story is told of the washer woman who worked for a man who was mean and cruel. Listening to a Christian radio program one afternoon she was wonderfully converted. From that day on she was incredibly happy, life was really worth living. Her boss did not give her leg-room and constantly ridiculed and belittled her. He gave her a hard time.

One day, out of the blue, he said to her: 'Betty, you say you're saved. How does it feel to be saved?' She told him: 'Well, I don't believe I can explain it, but here's what it feels like to me—it feels as though I'm standing in Jesus' shoes and he is standing in mine!'

Many years after Paul's time, Count Nicolaus Ludwig von Zinzendorf (1700-60) expressed the same truth in these words:

Jesus, thy blood and righteousness
My beauty are, my glorious dress;
'Midst flaming worlds, in these arrayed,
With joy shall I lift up my head.

3:10, 11

To know him and make him known

When Paul reached the point in his life of surrender to Jesus Christ he edges forward in his desire to know God intimately. Paul has seen so many folks who were content to live their lives on the low road. Not him. He is taking the high road. Charles Simeon said that whenever he looked at the portrait of the Cambridge honours graduate, Henry Martyn, who died in India at thirty-one years of age, that the words 'Don't trifle! Don't trifle!' always hit him like a bolt from the blue.

Like Martyn, the mediocre, humdrum, run-of-the-mill, ordinary life is not even entertained in Paul's mind for a moment. He is jumping on the springboard in his attempt to reach higher heights with the Lord. Here is the heart cry of a man earnestly seeking after God. He longed for Jesus, simply Jesus—nothing more. Paul says: 'Lord, I want to know you better! Lord, I want to know you more and more!'

It took him a wee while to get there for it did not happen overnight. There are no instant results when it comes to true spirituality. We cannot snap our fingers and demand it as if we were waiting for a meal in a restaurant where the service is at a snail's pace. Someone has said that 'heaven never hangs out the sign: Overnight Transformations. Enquire Within.'

Paul was a thinker, a man with a quick brain and razor-sharp analytical mind. He was also a theologian, a man with a warm and effusive heart. If the truth be told, neither fully satisfied the cravings of his inner man. That is what makes his personal vision statement all the more remarkable for this is how Paul wants to spend the rest of his life.

Paul writes: *I want to know (ginōskō) Christ and the power (dynamis) of his resurrection (anastasis) and the fellowship of sharing (koinōnia) in his sufferings (pathēma), becoming like (symmorphizō) him in his death (thanatos), and so, somehow, to attain (katantaō) to the resurrection (exanastasis) from the dead (nekros).*

Graham Kendrick captured the sentiment of Paul's desire in the words of his beautiful song:

All I once held dear, built my life upon,
All this world reveres, and wants to own,
All I once thought gain, I have counted loss;
Spent and worthless now, compared to this.

Knowing you, Jesus, knowing you,
There is no greater thing.
You're my all, you're the best,
You're my joy, my righteousness,
And I love you, Lord.

In the know

Paul's continuing aim is *to know him.* It is a goal that he is resolutely seeking after. It is the all-consuming passion—the throbbing ambition—of his life. Yes, he came to know the Lord on the Damascus highway when Jesus appeared to him in a bolt of white fire and spoke to him in person. That intrusion was okay for starters. However, Paul wants this to be more than a casual, polite relationship. Much more. He wants to be connected in an experiential way—something empirical.

A mother ran into the bedroom when she heard her son scream and found his two-year-old sister pulling his hair. She gently released the little girl's grip and said comfortingly to her son: 'There, darling, she didn't mean it. She doesn't know that it hurts when she pulls your hair.' The mother was barely out of the room when she heard the little girl cry. Rushing back into the room, she asked: 'What happened?'

Her son said: 'She knows now!'

It is not the *know* of intellect, but the *know* of intimacy.

Leaving gender issues aside, we know the Prime Minister of the United Kingdom—that is, we know his name, we know who he is, but very few of us know him personally. Most of us will be aware of the President of the USA—that is, we know who he is, but even fewer among us would claim to know him one-on-one as a person. That is the mega difference between knowing someone and *really* knowing someone.

I agree with Joe Stowell when he writes: 'The distance between knowing him and knowing about him is vast. And the space between these two experiences separates the spectators from intimate participants.'

But and Ben

In the idyllic and rustic setting of the Highlands and Islands of Bonnie Scotland, many of the traditional crofts have two rooms—a 'but' and a 'ben'. No matter who it was came to the front door, they would be automatically shown into the but. There were some notable exceptions to that general rule. When a special friend called to visit, they would be taken into the ben.

You see, there is a difference in the relationship, but not in the warmth of the highland welcome. That is why you would often hear the crofters saying among themselves, rather softly and quaintly: 'I see you were far ben with so-and-so.'

Paul says: 'I want to be far ben with God!'

There is an old hymn penned by Eliza Edmunds Hewitt (1851-1920) which sums this aspiration up very well:

More about Jesus would I know,
More of his grace to others show;
More of his saving fulness see,
More of his love who died for me.

More, more about Jesus!
Tell me more about Jesus!
More of his saving fulness see,
More of his love who died for me.

Superpower

We have known the *power of his resurrection* in the past—at the precise moment of our conversion we were raised up with Christ and seated in heavenly places (*cf.* Ephesians 2:6). We can know that power in today's world for Christ's resurrection was accomplished so that we might 'live a new life' (Romans 6:4). We will know that power completely in the future when our bodies will be raised up just as his was (*cf.* 1 Corinthians 15:52). Such power 'will kick-start an eternity of unhindered joy in our fellowship with Jesus,' suggests Joe Stowell.

The dynamic of God is an unleashing of eternal energy in your life and mine. Make no mistake, resurrection power is dynamite. Spiritual semtex. It has all the explosive potential to blow our minds and enable us to maximise the potency of God in our lives. We need to live—must live—24/7 in the *power of his resurrection*. The stone is rolled away!

There is no need for us to be trounced when we engage the enemy. We go forward in the illustrious triumph of Jesus. We fight the adversary from the position of victory. This is not salvation that Paul is talking about here, albeit it is coming out of the bonds of death into newness of life—a kind of spiritual awakening—but this is a daily awareness of the resurrection in our experience of God.

In ourselves, as Paul hinted earlier, we can do nothing, we are nothing, we have nothing. So often we fail to adequately cope with the harrowing conflicts of this life, we find it enormously difficult to conquer the binding habits of sin, it is a constant struggle for us to live lives of purity and holiness. The way to do it—the only way to do it—is for us to draw on the plenteous resources we have in Jesus Christ, that is, his risen life. We are alive unto God!

It was a dream come true for the Frenchman who became an Englishman because he so admired the Brits way of life. An inquisitive friend asked him what significant difference his British citizenship had made to him. Pierre replied: 'Well, among other things, I find that now, instead of losing the Battle of Waterloo, I've won it!'

The power of the resurrection makes us winners! Believe it or not, the same power that God used to raise Jesus from the dead is available to everyone of us. Make sure your life is plugged in and switched on. In this context, God wants us to be power hungry.

Something to share

Did you notice how Paul phrased his prayer? He used the word *sharing*. In Christ's joys and triumphs, in his love and grace, in his many blessings ... yes! But that was not what Paul prayed. He openly talks about *sharing in his sufferings*.

Actually, he says more, for he describes this as *fellowship*. I am afraid our perception of fellowship is often from a slightly different perspective than this. Having said that, it really is a genuine privilege for us to suffer for him—to bear the scars of battle, to know the pangs that rend the human heart, to feel the pain that torments the body, to encounter the anguish that affliction brings, to reel under the chilling wind of adversity—that is fellowship with him in his sufferings. It means a cross.

The trials of life. Troublesome times. Turbulent days. Tumultuous moments. What an amazing honour to think that the Lord counts us worthy to face them. You may not have seen it like that before but that is fellowship with a capital F. And suffering is one of those places where our tiny world and his intersects. In fellowship, we have to capitalise on where our world merges with his.

When meditating on these truths, Charles Wesley (1707-88) put pen to paper and wrote these words:

Thy love for a sinner declare,
Thy passion and death on the tree;
My spirit to Calvary bear,
To suffer and triumph with thee.

It entails each of us taking up and bearing the cross in our lives. A painful experience. It may hurt. It could sting. Sore. It takes undiluted commitment for there is a price to pay and it may cost us dear. We may be the butt of cynical jokes. Perhaps subject to ridicule or even prone to ostracism. Possibly misunderstood. There is a reproach that has to be willingly and gladly borne for the sake of Jesus.

Dead and alive

The order that Paul outlines in his prayer is significant—he moves from a resurrection, to a sacrifice, to a death. On the face of it, it appears to be back to front, almost like putting the cart before the horse. The bottom line: we cannot have a resurrection without a death. So, Paul says, *becoming like him in his death.* This is a dying daily to self, sin, and Satan.

When we die to each of these 'big three' influences in our lives then we become fully alive in Jesus. It is when 'I' is dethroned and Christ is enthroned. It is when 'I' is crucified and Christ is crowned. It is only when the corn of wheat falls into the ground and dies that it bears much fruit (*cf.* John 12:24).

That is why Jesus came. Calvary was the aim of the incarnation. He was born to die. Then he died to live. The same can be true in our lives if we are willing to sign our name on the dotted line and wholeheartedly endorse the sentiments so movingly expressed by Paul: 'Lord, I want to know you!'

Beyond these walls

This is the only place in the New Testament where this form of the Greek word for *resurrection* is used. Literally, it means 'out resurrection'—the resurrection 'out from the dead ones'.

When the dead in Christ rise at the coming again of our Lord Jesus, the next scheduled event on God's prophetic calendar is the rewarding of the people of God at the judgment seat of Christ (*cf.* Romans 14:12; 1 Corinthians 3:10-15; 2 Corinthians 5:10). Paul was speaking of that moment when he would stand before his Lord and Saviour. He definitely did not want to appear red-faced and empty-handed. He wanted to be able to offer to him fruit rather than leaves.

It was Paul's hope and desire that at this particular time he might receive a reward for his unflagging pursuit of the knowledge of Jesus Christ. In order to receive that reward in the next life, he would have to *attain* or earn it in this life. Part of that reward, it seems to me, is the inherent ability to know Christ on the other side of death.

It all harks back to the decisive hour in Paul's life when he realised the arrant fallacy of being driven by confidence in the flesh as it was only taking him into a dead-end street, a spiritual cul-de-sac. A defining moment. Indeed.

Paul quickly found that his religion was just like an onion.

When he peeled away layer upon layer of traditions, rules, and regulations, he discovered to his out-and-out horror that he had nothing. Sweet Fanny Adams! On the other hand, Paul found that Christianity was like a treasure chest. The outside may have looked fairly unimpressive, but when he opened it and looked inside he was pleasantly surprised, if not taken aback. He found a cross, an empty tomb, a promise of power, a hope of glory, and riches beyond measure—all embodied in one person— the Lord Jesus Christ. Paul could happily identify with the observation of W. H. Griffith Thomas when he noted that 'Christianity is nothing less and can be nothing more than relationship to Christ.'

Charles Swindoll says that 'Paul wanted to spend the balance of his years on earth …

- knowing Christ more intimately,
- drawing upon his resurrection power more increasingly,
- entering into his sufferings more personally, and
- being conformed to his image more completely.'

Mark Prendergrass summed it up well when he wrote:

The greatest thing in all my life is knowing you,
The greatest thing in all my life is knowing you,
I want to know you more, I want to know you more.
The greatest thing in all my life is knowing you.

I cannot help but ask myself the question: 'Am I staying too near where I got in?' Maybe you should ask the same!

3:12, 13a

Going for gold

That is the aim and aspiration of the vast company of athletes who assemble every four years from all over the world to take part in the Olympics. For them to stand on the winner's podium, hailed as heroes, with the strains of their home country's national anthem ringing in their ears, emotion etched on their tear-stained faces, would make all the sacrifice and strenuous effort worthwhile.

It seems to me that the Christian life is no different. Paul sees it as a race—it is not a 100-metre dash—it is more like a marathon cross-country. Of necessity, we are to abandon our own selfish ambitions so that we may enthusiastically pursue the goal that is set before us. Nothing must hinder or hamper our steady progress. It is not a spectator sport but one of active participation by all. Down the straight, round the bend, over the hurdle, in the final analysis, consistency is what really matters.

There will be wave after wave of frustration as we strive to attain spiritual fitness. Many tears may be shed as we count the cost of getting rid of the excess baggage. The pain barrier must be broken if we are to keep on going. But even though we may not all be winners by nature, with the spiritual instincts of the new man reigning within, we can conquer all and cross the finishing line in triumph.

Awaiting us is Christ, the one who has gone on before. No greater incentive can be given. No other motivation should be needed. That is why we pull out all the stops, with every fibre of our being, stretching all the sinews, as we keep the end in view. What an exhilarating prospect. Going for gold, and God.

This was Paul's philosophy. His game plan. Fair play, he stuck rigidly to it. Like him, we want to be there at the end.

'Destiny is not a matter of chance, it is a matter of choice. It is not a thing to be waited for, it is a thing to be achieved.' (William Jennings Bryan)

Paul shows us how to do it in 3:12-16 by leaving us a few top tips designed to enhance our performance:

- be realistic—know where you are at,
- be focused—learn the art of concentration,
- be forward-looking—resist the temptation to look back,
- be a plodder—no need to drop out on the last lap,
- be sensible—know the rules and stick to them.

Winning moves. Yes. Absorb them. Get yourself down to the track. Success—everybody wants it, the problem is no one wants to pay for it. At a recent seminar, I gulped when I heard it said that a successful executive in business is the person who delegates all the responsibility, shifts all the blame, and gets all the credit. An Irishman told me one day that 'success is getting your mother-in-law to go home early!'

A touch of realism

Paul is brutally honest when he writes about his apparent lack of success: *Not that I have already obtained (lambanō) all this, or have already been made perfect (teleioō), but I press on (diōkō) to take hold (katalambanō) of that for which Christ Jesus took hold of me. Brothers, I do not consider myself yet to have taken hold of it.*

If the old adage is true that open confession is good for the soul, Paul will feel a lot better for having cleared his chest. He comes clean and we can hardly believe what he says. It is a frank assessment of where he is at spiritually. Here is honesty clothed in humility.

Paul has not arrived. He has not reached his goal. He has not achieved his cherished ambition. What a fantastic relief to find that Paul has similar struggles to the rest of us lesser mortals. Perfection eludes us. It cannot be any other way.

We live in a seriously imperfect world. We are surrounded by imperfect people. We witness a legion of imperfections on a daily basis in every area of modern life. And the bitter-sweet news is that it will continue in that vein until we reach heaven itself.

It is quite remarkable when we realise that, at this juncture, the apostle Paul was at the zenith of his career and, even there, he admits he has not reached the high-water mark of his calling. Here is the dude who permeated major cities with the gospel, who founded churches which continue to flourish, who wrote ten major doctrinal letters which even today astound biblical scholars, and he is not satisfied with himself. Correct.

It seems the more Paul accomplished, the more he saw that needed to be accomplished. Not for him the easy way out of putting his feet up on a pouf and resting on his laurels. We do not find Paul reclining on a plush leather chair, listening to classical music, and doing the crossword, all bathed in a heady air of smug complacency.

The picture here is of a man who is far from content with his progress on the road that leads to Christ-likeness. I mean, Paul honestly admits that he is not perfect! There was room for improvement. Lots of room. There was still plenty of scope for advancement in many departments of his life. He has no will-o'-the-wisp feelings about himself, nor is he under any phantasmagoria when it comes to future growth in grace. He knows full well there is a long, long way to go.

'Success is not determined by what we are but rather by what we are compared to what we could be. It is not measured by what we have done but rather by what we have done compared to what we could have done.' (James Merritt)

Paul says: 'Look, folks, this is where I am … that is where I am going … and, in between, I have a lot to learn.' The motto of Spurgeon's College, London is *Teneo et Teneor*, that is: 'I hold and I am held.'

3:13b

Be single-minded

The temptation we all grapple with is to have too many irons in the fire at the same time. We were never meant to be a Jack-of-all-trades. God wants us to be master of one. Hence Paul's incisive comment: *But one (heis) thing I do!*

Concentration is essential. It is the name of the game. We should be immersed in one thing and invest our energy towards its final accomplishment. We should be keen to see it through to the end and not let anyone or anything distract us. So much crowds into our lives that this *one thing* has been crowded out.

Remember Nehemiah on the building site in Jerusalem. This was the spirit he portrayed when he reacted to people who wanted to waste his time. He said: 'I am doing a great work so that I cannot come down' (Nehemiah 6:3). It is all about being focused and having the ability to home in on the target with precision and dedication. If we have too many irons in the fire, there are two options open to us: one, we take some out and, two, we extinguish the fire.

D L Moody is credited with the statement: 'It is better to say, "this one thing I do" than to say, "these forty things I dabble in".' Many people tinker or putter around with much, but succeed at nothing. Despite all the energy they expend, they have precious little to show for it. Instead of our lives being like a bullet fired from a rifle towards a single goal, we are like buckshot from a shotgun spread all over the place.

We can be single-minded without being narrow-minded.

At the end of the day, it is a matter of personal values, of getting our priorities right, of sorting out the agenda of our lives. Maybe we need to take to heart Austen Farrer's advice and 'do fewer things and do them better.' We need to always remember that the most important thing is to ensure that the most important thing remains the most important thing.

Keep looking ahead

The phrase that Paul employs—*forgetting (epilanthanomai) what is behind (opisō)*—is one that is borrowed from the world of athletics. It was used of a runner who outran another in the same race. Once he got into the lead, he would never turn and look back. In that sense, he forgets about the other competitors in the race. He focuses only on the tape that is before him.

Sporting enthusiasts of a certain vintage will never forget that memorable mile race at the Empire Games in Vancouver many years ago when John Landy, the Australian champion, looked back over his left shoulder to see where Roger Bannister was, only for Bannister to pass him on his right.

What a galvanising challenge! We cannot afford to live our lives looking back over our shoulders. The past is behind us and it cannot be changed. Whether we like it or not, we cannot rewrite the history of our lives. It happened yesterday and we should be content to leave it there. We can all learn from the past, sure we can. But the man is a fool who tries to live in the past. Winston Churchill was right when he said: 'If the present is quarrelling with your past, there can be no future.'

I heard about the little fellow who was listening to his Sunday School teacher tell about Lot's wife and how she looked back and turned into a pillar of salt. 'That's nothing,' he piped up, 'my mum was driving the car yesterday and she looked back and turned into a telegraph pole.'

Forget it!

The apostle encourages us to forget about our past failures. So often when we think about them we plunge into the dark depths of despair and become defeatist in our outlook. The past can—and sometimes does—give us a mental block. It can colour our perception of the present and taint our better sense of judgment. It can so easily shackle us and lead us into bondage. It has been said that 'memory is a nursery where grown children play with broken toys.'

Instead of the past being a useful instrument to teach us beneficial lessons, it can all too quickly become an enervating influence that terrorises us. If we are going to be successful in our quest for gold we need to stay in the right lane and on the right track—a walk into the past will only succeed in derailing and demoralising us. Such memories haunt us, not help us.

The story is told of the businessman who was notorious for saving everything that came across his desk. Invariably the office files were bulging. One day his PA asked if she might dispose of the old material. He was reluctant but finally he said: 'OK, Mary, but make sure you make a copy of everything before you shred it and throw it away.'

It is equally true to say that we should also forget about our past successes. If we do not, it would be dangerously easy for us to become slick and overconfident and relax our spiritual training program. Grateful.

Yes! Proud. No! We cannot live on the tantalising blessing of yesterday's triumphs. Today is another day, a day with lots of new challenges and loads of fresh opportunities. If we are genuinely going for gold, we will not flinch from steadfastly looking ahead.

Timothy Dudley-Smith penned these words:

Lord, for ourselves; in living power remake us,
Self on the cross and Christ upon the throne,
Past put behind us, for the future take us:
Lord of our lives, to live for Christ alone.

Someone once asked Scottish missionary and explorer David Livingstone (1813-73) when he was back in England briefly after having worked for many years in Africa: 'Well, Dr Livingstone, where are you ready to go now?' Like a flash, the not-so-easily-put-off Dr Livingstone answered: 'I am ready to go anywhere, provided it be forward!'

The parting shot: if we keep remembering our successes, we will soon have nothing to remember.

3:13c, 14

Keep plodding on

Straining (epekteinomai) towards what is ahead (emprosthen), I press (diōkō) on towards the goal (skopos) to win the prize (brabeion) for which God has called (klēsis) me heavenwards (anō) in Christ Jesus. The chances are when Paul drafted these words that he had a picture in his mind's eye of the chariot races that were so popular in the Olympic Games.

Charles Swindoll reckons that 'he could have been thinking of the charioteer standing in that small, two-wheeled cart with long leather reins in his hands, leaning forward to keep his balance.'

Definitely not a sport for the timorous or fainthearted among us. It was only for those willing to risk life and limb in order to claim the garland at the end of the race. Nevertheless, such should be our experience of life—we are to keep our eyes pinpointed directly ahead of us in anticipation of the day when we cross the finishing line. From here to there, the best line to follow is that of our putting everything into it. Anything less than our best will result in our coming unstuck. Frankly, that is too high a price to pay.

Another fascinating simile adopted by Paul is his use of the terms: *to take hold of ... took hold of me.* It is the picture of the rugby league player who runs someone down from behind and tackles him so that he might get his hands on the ball. Paul wanted to experience everything that God had for his life and he was eager to grab hold of all that God put in front of him.

We also detect in the phrase, *pressing on towards the goal,* an allusion to a track athlete. The verb reminds us of someone who runs without swerving off course, straining every nerve and muscle as he keeps on running with all his might towards the goal.

Whichever comparison you may prefer to personalise, all that matters is that we keep on going to the very end of the race. Sadly too many fall out on the last lap. For one reason or another, they drop out and fail to finish. It all becomes too much for them. Losers.

Crossing the finishing line

When weariness invades our bodies, when the pain barrier needs to be crossed, when the odds are stacked even higher than the hurdles, when we are hurt in the fray at the many bends on track, when we are elbowed and lose our wind for a time, when we are spiked and spill blood in the process, when we trip and fall in the dust—we must keep on going.

In the 1968 Olympic Games held in Mexico City, marathon runner John Stephen Akhware of Tanzania staggered into the stadium more than an hour after the winner had crossed the line. His right leg was bloody and bandaged—he was in a bad way. At the post-race press conference, his comment to the world's media echoed his nonpareil commitment when he said: 'My country didn't send me to Mexico City to start the race. They sent me to finish the race!'

Why? It is all about securing the glittering prize at the end of the race. In life, as in any sport, we will not go far unless we know where the goalposts are. It is the award that makes it eminently worthwhile. The victor's wreath. A congratulatory word of praise and commendation. A gleaming crown that never fades. This is the sole reason for our calling in God—heavenly, holy, and high as it is.

At the Greek games, the winner of a race was summoned from the stadium floor to the elevated seat (the bema) of the official umpire. A wreath of leaves was placed upon his head. At Athens, the winner was also given five hundred coins, free meals, and a front row seat at the theatre.

In Paul's thinking, the goal and the prize converge. They are one and the same—Jesus!

3:15, 16

Keep your cool

Paul's insightful remarks in these verses are nothing more than old-fashioned common sense. But, if your experience is akin to mine, sense is not very common these days. Paul says we should abide by the rules and not seek to find a way around them. If we want to hold our heads up high as we breast the tape then obedience to the rules is absolutely essential. We should never seek to infringe the guidelines set out before us.

Tell me: who wants to be disqualified? who wants to be shown the red card? who wants to walk the tunnel of shame? who wants to take an early bath?

All of us who are mature (teleios) should take such a view of things (phroneō). And if on some point you think differently (heterōs), that too God will make clear (apokalyptō) to you. Only let us live up to what we have already attained.

Reality hits us between the eyes when we realise that the track is littered with people who began the race with enormous potential and ended up being disqualified because they broke the rules. Simply not worth it.

I recall the likes of Lot, Samson, Saul, Ananias, Sapphira, and Demas, to name but a few. O yes, they were competing, it is just that they were in a different race. They were left with a crimson red face and their head buried in their hands.

This is the policy Paul adhered to and which he feels strongly is the line that mature believers should also take on board. There will be those who have other ideas. There always is. Paul is happy to agree to differ with them because he knows that God will have the last word. He always does.

The final sentence in verse 16 is a timely challenge to all those in the church at Philippi (and since then) not to throw out the baby with the bath water. They have come so far. They have done so well. They have made up a lot of ground. They have everything to live for.

Says Paul: 'Don't be foolish and throw it all away in a mad moment of reckless abandon!' They would be crazy people if they allowed themselves to become sidetracked at such a critical moment. The finishing line would disappear over the horizon and they would be the ultimate losers. They are to persevere with gritted teeth and honest endeavour.

Head down. Eyes front. Moving forward. One step at a time. In going for gold—they are going for God!

'Let's not settle for anything less than heaven wills to give us.' (Duncan Campbell)

At the foot of one of the Swiss Alps is a marker honouring a mountaineer who fell to his death attempting a steep ascent. The simple brass marker gives his name and this brief epitaph: 'He died climbing.' The epitaph of every Christian should be that they died climbing the upward path toward the ultimate prize of Christ-likeness. Johnson Oatman (1856-1926) wrote:

I'm pressing on the upward way,
New heights I'm gaining every day;
Still praying as I onward bound,
'Lord, plant my feet on higher ground.'

The story is told of William Borden, graduate of Yale and son of fabulously wealthy parents, that en route to China as a missionary he contracted a fatal disease and died. At his bedside, his friends found a scribbled note that he had penned a few hours before his death. On that piece of paper were the words: 'No reserve, no retreat, and no regrets!'

3:17

Character check

'You can tell the character of a man by what it takes to stop him.'
(Anonymous)

Of course that statement needs some qualification for we need to make sure that a person's objectives are worthy before we talk about the toughness of character that keeps them going, no matter what. The fact is that some good men could have been great men if they had not stopped so soon.

Though we often see cowardice in the lives of others, it is not so easily detected in ourselves. It is the 'speck of sawdust in your brother's eye and the plank in your own eye' syndrome.

Apparently in one of his long speeches to the Supreme Soviet, Nikita Khrushchev (1894-1971) was severely critical of Joseph Stalin (1879-1953) to such an extent that someone from the floor of the hall sent up a note to the Premier to read. Its caustic message came in the form of a question: 'What were you doing when Stalin committed all those atrocities?'

'Who sent up this note?' Khrushchev shouted.

Not a person stirred. There was an eerie silence.

'I'll give him one minute to stand up!'

Still no one moved as the seconds ticked away. Time was fast running out.

'All right, I'll tell you what I was doing,' Khrushchev began. 'I was doing what the writer of this note was doing—nothing! I was afraid to be counted!'

Paul was a man who was willing to be counted. He could not be stopped. He had a dozen reasons why he could have chosen an early retirement. He could have spent his twilight years writing his memoirs. But he did not. Why? Because he had a goal in view. He had a sense of destiny. He was on a mission and the job was still not done. He never lost his vision, it never became blurred.

Warren Wiersbe describes Paul as:

- an accountant with a new set of values (*cf.* 3:1-11),
- an athlete with vigour and vitality (*cf.* 3:12-16), and
- an alien with a fresh vision (*cf.* 3:17-21).

What does this man of A-OK vision have to say to us as we engage a postmodern world in the third millennium?

Role model

Join with others in following my example (symmimētēs), brothers, and take note (skopeō) of those who live according to the pattern (typos) we gave you. Brave man. Courageous man. Indeed. Paul is not being foolhardy at this point. Nor is he showing signs of audacity and brashness. He is definitely not on an ego trip to increase the measurement of his head. All he says is: 'Do as I do!' and 'Do as I say!'

Maturity proceeds through four stages:

- stage one: help me,
- stage two: tell me,
- stage three: show me,
- stage four: follow me.

That is where Paul is right now—stage four. He is encouraging them to mimic his example. If they do, their lives will be the better for it. They need to keep on walking with God, keep on growing in Christ, keep on climbing in their pursuit of holiness. They are not alone for many others are with them on the pilgrimage. A journey of joy. His example is not the only one worth imitating, there are plenty of others whose lives can be admired and appreciated.

His was a lifestyle worth duplicating, an example worth copying. It would be so good for them to see him as a role model. They would retain their sense of personal identity, and not become a shadow of someone else. He was not expecting them to become replicas in Philippi of himself. They would hold on to their individual personalities but each of them would be marching to the drumbeat of Jesus. Oddly enough, they would find Paul in step to the same tune.

Men followers. Maybe. In following Paul, however, they were walking in the footsteps of Jesus. As they followed the missionaries, so they followed the Master. The reason why Paul was able to give them such a gentle nudge was because of his closeness to Christ, his communion with Christ, and his consecration to Christ.

His conduct was exemplary. O that we were able to say the same to our peers as Paul said to his. It is impossible to assess the power of a godly example. H W Longfellow was on the same wavelength when he penned the words:

Lives of great men all remind us
We can make our lives sublime,
And, departing, leave behind us
Footprints on the sands of time.

Footprints, that perhaps another,
Sailing o'er life's solemn main,
A forlorn and shipwrecked brother,
Seeing, shall take heart again.

When the British mountaineers, George Mallory and Andrew Irvine, were lost from sight near the summit of Everest in 1924, their companions beneath them reported to base camp that they were 'last seen still climbing'. What an accolade—may that be true of us all.

3:18, 19

Blacklisted

We caught a fleeting glimpse of Paul in verse 17 as a brave man, now we see him as a broken man with tears in his eyes. The preacher is weeping— he is overcome with emotion as his heart rends at the prospect of some of the members of the church at Philippi becoming ensnared with a first-century personality cult. No wonder he writes: *For, as I have often told you before and now say again even with tears (klaiō), many live as enemies (echthros) of the cross of Christ.*

Paul breaks down as he contemplates the dissolute bleakness of these pseudo-saints. They are synthetic saints and spiritual masquerades. They look genuine, but lack reality. They pose as friends, but practice as foes—they are enemies.

There were two groups of tricksters who surreptitiously infiltrated the ranks of the early church—the Judaisers and the Antinomians. Their policies are fairly straightforward and can be summarised in a few words. The Judaisers are the party of the law where nothing goes. The Antinomians are renowned as the party of liberty where anything and everything goes.

Paul says three things about them in the following verse: *Their destiny (telos) is destruction (apōleia), their god (theos) is their stomach (koilia), and their glory (doxa) is in their shame (aischynē). Their mind (phroneō) is on earthly (epigeios) things.*

Harbinger of doom

What an awful end awaits those who know not Jesus as Lord and Saviour. This is their future. Eternal hopelessness. Hell. Wasted lives. Irredeemable lostness. Never-ending darkness. Their goal is perdition—damnation—where they are banished from the presence of a holy and just God forever. Such is the terrifying fate of those who are mere professors with an empty religion.

Hedonism

People of this ilk are totally wrapped up in themselves and have immersed their lives in sordid fleshly affairs. They worship at the shrine of their pleasures. They are driven by an insatiable sensual appetite and have no hangups about their lack of moral purity. They are totally absorbed in a rigid regime of dietary laws as they pamper themselves and pander to their every whim and fancy.

They are carnal and corrupt, flaunting their sexuality. Their lives revolve around matters of time and the insistence on doing their own thing. They have a perverted sense of values as sensuality is the fuel that lights their fire. They are big on erotica.

A penchant for ...

To me this is the telltale factor. Everyone has a grid or mindset through which he makes major life decisions. That grid determines what happens next. Outlook determines outcome. Paul's grid was heaven, theirs was the earth. They are earthed to this present world—earth dwellers, earth bound, and earth orientated. They were materialistic and could see no further than the here and now. Their view was all soil and no sky.

They are like the man with the muck rake in John Bunyan's *Pilgrims Progress* who never looked up, or like the man described by Alexander Maclaren who kept heaping up the dust of the condemned cell and calling it gold.

3:20, 21

Resident aliens

The contrast between them and us is seen in Paul's use of the word *but* at the beginning of verse 20: *But our citizenship (politeuma) is in heaven (epouranios). And we eagerly await (apekdechomai) a Saviour (Sōtēr) from there, the Lord Jesus Christ, who, by the power (energeia) that enables (dynamai) him to bring everything under his control (hypotassō), will transform (metaschēmatizō) our lowly (tapeinōsis) bodies (sōma) so that they will be like his glorious (doxa) body.*

We live on planet earth but we really belong to another world. We pitch the tent of our life down here but we are not getting our roots down. We are just passing through as this world is not our home. We are only here as temporary tenants as our main residence is in heaven.

A young woman completing a job application came to the line asking for her permanent address. She began to list her street and house number, but paused for a moment. Then, with a small smile she wrote one word: Heaven. A famous medical missionary to China, Dr Duncan Main, was told that the Chinese equivalent of his name was: 'Dr Apricot of Heaven Below!'

We are not vagabonds, without a home. Neither are we fugitives, on the run from home. We are pilgrims, we have a home. Up there.

Settlers. *No!* Pilgrims in transit. *Yes!*

A colony of heaven

We are here and, at the same time, we are there. We are in two places at once. The locals would be familiar with such a helpful analogy as Philippi was looked on as a military colony of Rome. The city was given that particular honour by the Emperor after a momentous military victory in 42 BC when Octavian and Mark Antony defeated the rebel forces of Brutus and Cassius—the assassins of Julius Caesar. Even further back the town took its name from the father of Alexander the Great, Philip II of Macedon, who captured the city from the Thracians in 360 BC.

Originally it was a Phoenician mining town because of its close proximity to gold mines located in the mountains and on the island of Thasos. Nowhere outside Italy was there any city more thoroughly Roman. It had been granted the high honour of the *ius Italicum*, that is, of being governed by Roman law. To all intents and purposes, it was Rome in miniature.

The inhabitants of Philippi were seen as Roman citizens even though Rome was a considerable distance from them. The same can be said for the people of God—we are here but, in reality, we belong elsewhere.

Pace-setters

This is the pioneer spirit that captivated the imagination and harnessed the energy of so many who have gone on before us. I think of father Abraham who looked for a city and was as pleased as Punch to live in a Bedouin tent. When he started out on his odyssey of discovery he left no forwarding address (*cf.* Hebrews 11:8).

Moses springs to mind as one who looked for the rewards of heaven and, because of that, he had no hangups turning his back on the treasures of Egypt (*cf.* Hebrews 11:24-26).

- He saw the invisible,
- he chose the imperishable, and

* he did the impossible.

The supreme example is our Lord Jesus Christ who, because of the joy that was before him, was willing to endure the horrors of Calvary (*cf.* Hebrews 12:2). That, in a nutshell, is the ethos of biblical Christianity—we have an eye on the future. Because of that, we should be ready to strike camp and move on at a moment's notice. Jesus is coming again. Soon. Suddenly. Surely.

I read about a Sunday School teacher who was teaching her class about the knockout wonders of heaven. When she finished, she asked: 'Class, how many of you want to go to heaven?' All the children raised their hand except Billy. The teacher asked him: 'Billy, don't you want to go to heaven?' He replied: 'Yes, I'd like to, but my mum told me to come straight home after church!'

When it comes to heaven, there should be a dash of vim and gusto in our outlook with our hearts beating faster every passing day. His advent is imminent. Each day is one day nearer. Each step is one step closer. Jesus could break through the clouds at any moment and we will want to be ready to meet him.

Going, going, gone

Jesus is coming from *there* to here for each of us who know him personally. He is returning so that he might take us me to heaven to spend the aeons of eternity in his immediate close presence. This is phase one of the advent program of Jesus Christ—when the Lord comes to the air for his redeemed people (*cf.* 1 Thessalonians 4:13-18).

In the driving seat

Phase two of his advent timetable is when, at the end of the period of Tribulation, the Lord returns to earth with his people. Jesus is coming to rule and reign. He will be seen to exercise sovereign control over the entire world—his enemies will become his footstool, he will crush the opposition, he will subdue all the tyranny of evil, and the earth will become his kingdom (*cf.* Matthew 24).

God's designer label

The unchanging Christ will, in that day when the trumpet sounds, become the all-changing Christ as he treats each of us to a divine makeover. In a moment, faster than the batting of an eyelid, we will be like Jesus. Tremendous.

Writing in a similar vein to the church at Corinth, the apostle said that our bodies will be buried in decay and raised without decay, sown in humiliation and raised in splendour, sown in weakness and raised in strength, sown a physical body and raised a spiritual body (*cf.* 1 Corinthians 15:42, 43).

The story is told of the country yokel and his redneck son who went to the big city for the very first time. They had never been off the farm and both were gobsmacked at all the things they saw. But the thing that most amazed the old farmer was an elevator.

They were standing in the lobby of a downtown building when they saw this old wrinkled, dishevelled woman on a walker step into the elevator. The door closed and, in a few minutes, it opened and out stepped this gorgeous looking young woman.

The farmer said to his son: 'Hey, son, wait right here. I'm going home to get your mamma and run her through that thing!'

One of these days, in God's good and perfect time, we are going to be transformed. He will give us a real body, a redeemed body, and a recognisable body. For, I believe, we shall know each other in heaven and we shall know as we are known. Then, and not before, the outstandingly 'good work' begun at the moment of our conversion will be complete (*cf.* 1:6). Wrote James Montgomery (1771-1854):

Here in the body pent,
Absent from him I roam,
Yet nightly pitch my moving tent,
A day's march nearer home.

What a vision Paul has of the fabulous future for believers. What a breathtaking vista he gives us of the unfolding purpose of God. It is probably right and proper that we should pause for a moment and pray with John on the Isle of Patmos: 'Amen. Come, Lord Jesus' (Revelation 22:20). That explains why Paul lived his life in the future tense. Homesick for heaven.

And that realisation means Paul is cognisant of his ongoing responsibilities in his present environment. We are here because God has placed us here. And until he comes and takes us out of this world, we have an obligation resting on our shoulders to reach those whom he calls the *enemies of the cross of Christ.* Lord Shaftesbury, the great English social reformer, said near the end of his life: 'I do not think that in the last forty years I have lived one conscious hour that was not influenced by the thought of our Lord's return.'

A story about Oliver Cromwell illustrates what God wants us to do in the time that is left to us prior to the second coming of Jesus. At the time, England was running out of silver for making coins. So the resourceful Cromwell sent his men to the cathedrals to see if they could find any silver there. They reported: *'The only silver we could find is in the statues of the saints standing in the corners!'* To which the crusty statesman replied: *'Good! We'll melt down the saints and put them into circulation!'*

Strategically, that is where we all belong—in circulation. Our place is not in the dimly lit corner of a musty church building, gathering dust. Our niche is out there among people. We have a message worth sharing. We have a mandate from heaven. We have an unfinished mission. We are the people God is looking to so that the great task of reaching a world without Jesus might progress with rapid speed.

There are some people who look at the way things are and ask: Why? Other people look at the way things could be and say: Why not? In light of Paul's immense challenge, where do you see yourself fitting in to the big picture?

God is calling us to be a *sunrise* people—dreaming of the future! Not a *sunset* people—drooling over the past!

4
No peace like God's peace

Going Dutch!

A trip to Amsterdam is not complete without a visit to the internationally renowned Rijksmuseum, the treasure house of the Netherlands. For a few extra euros you can have the benefit of a tour guide with all his expertise. During the course of his running commentary, he will inform you of an amazing statistic that about ten percent of Rembrandt's paintings were paintings of himself. But far from being an exercise in self-aggrandisement, Rembrandt (1606-69) was a humble person who painted himself just as he was, with no embellishments.

Artists have often wondered why he did not take advantage of his gifted hand and paint himself with just a touch of flattery, since his physical form was far from handsome. But Rembrandt remarked: 'Unless I can paint myself just as I am, I cannot paint others as they are!'

In the previous three chapters of his epistle, we have seen the apostle in his true colours. Now, in this final chapter, he sketches a picture of life behind the walls in the first-century church at Philippi. Stroke after stroke on the canvas of Scripture, he paints it as it is.

There were people. Lots of them. And where we have people, we have problems. Lots more of them.

I love the rather personal story recounted by Warren Wiersbe: My daughter jumped off the school bus as it stopped in front of our house and slammed her way through the front door. She marched defiantly up the stairs into her room and again slammed the door. All the time she was muttering under her breath: 'People, people, people, PEOPLE!'

I went to her door and knocked softly. 'May I come in?'

She replied: 'No!'

I tried again, but she said it even more belligerently: 'No!'

I asked: 'Why can't I come in?'

Her answer: 'Because you're a people!'

People are problems

That kind of scene happens every day all across the country. In fact, it is probably happening at a home near you, right now. Ask any parent—they know exactly how Mr Wiersbe felt. Ask any child—they know exactly how his daughter felt. There are times when people can and do have that effect on us. It is most unpleasant.

In a *Peanuts* cartoon, Lucy says to Snoopy: *'There are times when you really bug me, but I must admit there are also times when I feel like giving you a big hug.'*

Snoopy replies: *'Lucy, that's the way I am—huggable and buggable!'*

So it is with many relationships in the local church family. It seems from reading between the lines that Philippi was no exception. There were tensions and, as these things go, people were taking sides. Fragmentation seemed inevitable. It is hard to comprehend that back in the first century when life was relatively simple and everyone's pace was so much slower that there were so many childish squabbles.

Sadly, some folks have nothing better to do with their time than waste it nitpicking and majoring on minors. To an outsider looking in, it all appears so embarrassingly petty. It is the sledgehammer to crack a nut syndrome that seemed so prevalent. It was all a wee bit over the top. It was needless and senseless.

Paul, in the next few verses, attempts to put out the raging fires that are blazing. He seeks to defuse the time bomb of disharmony. That is the root problem from which has sprung three main areas of pastoral concern.

4:1

A defeatist mentality

Paul has a wonderful way of describing people. He gives them a shot in the arm and that makes them feel good. He boosts their morale as he affirms them for who they are: *Therefore, my brothers, you whom I love (agapētos) and long for (epipothētos), my joy (chara) and crown (stephanos), that is how you should stand firm (histemi) in the Lord, dear friends!*

A quick look at the verse tells us that Paul speaks of them in a fourfold manner. He starts the ball rolling when he calls them *brothers (adelphos)* because they were all members of the same family. He looked upon them as his spiritual brothers and sisters. And they were.

A most interesting turn of phrase is used when Paul refers to them as *my joy.* This is a salubrious reminder to them of the tremendous joy they have brought into his life. So far as Paul is concerned, they are the icing on the cake of his Christian experience.

My ... crown is a reference to what they will be in a day to come. He has led them to the Lord and, at the judgment seat of Christ, he will receive a soul winner's crown. They will be the sparkling jewels in that crown. What a fitting reward for the man who was instrumental in their conversion.

Stress fractures

Paul unashamedly talks about them being his *dear friends* and this is suggestive of the love that binds their hearts together. The apostle is cheery and relaxed when sharing with them because he really enjoys their sweet fellowship—they mean so much to him.

He bares his heart when he tells them: *I love and long for [you]*. In other words, Paul values them as a people for who they are. He accepts them. He is enamoured with them and so the terms of endearment flow easily and naturally, both from his pen and his heart.

Having reassured them of his affection, he then proceeds to challenge them to *stand firm in the Lord*. Some of them were beginning to ping under the pressure they were encountering. They were on the verge of giving up and giving in. It would have been so easy for them to yield hard-won ground to the enemy. Retreat seemed a viable (and attractive) alternative as they thought to themselves: 'If we can't stand the heat, let's get out of the kitchen!' Looking at the overall situation from an objective perspective, these were all soft options.

The first signs of instability were beginning to appear as the dreaded cracks were making an unwelcome entry into the life and soul of the fellowship. There was a heavy air of gloom and despondency as one after another adopted a defeatist mentality. They were in the doldrums. Says Paul: *stand firm*.

Their power base is *in the Lord*. This particular expression is found no fewer than eight times in Paul's letter. Jesus is the secret of their strength and security. He is the source of their power.

All the way through Paul's note to the church, the focus has been not on our circumstances, or on others, or on ourselves, but on the living Lord. Their eyes should be looking only to him. He will enable them to get up and go on. If they pick up the broken pieces in their interpersonal relationships, he will put them back together again—they are family. And they are in it together.

This durable concept of 'standing firm' is one of Paul's hobbyhorses. He often writes along these lines. For example:

- 'stand firm in the faith' (*cf.* 1 Corinthians 16:13),
- 'stand firm in your freedom' (*cf.* Galatians 5:1),
- 'stand firm on your foundation' (*cf.* 2 Thessalonians 2:15).

In this verse, Paul reminds them to 'stand firm in the family'—together they can face the foe. They are on the winning team. Therefore, it is imperative that they be positive in their outlook. Victory is certain.

4:2, 3

Defusing the time bomb of disharmony

Here is public enemy number one and Paul puts his finger on it immediately. He calls a spade, a spade, not a sharp-edged gardening implement. Paul bravely tackles the thorny problem when he writes: *I plead (parakaleō) with Euodia and I plead with Syntyche to agree (phroneō) with each other in the Lord.*

Tragic. A fly in the ointment. Two ladies who should know better have a nuclear fallout. They are at loggerheads, at one another's throats. Something happened between them to sour their previously excellent working relationship. We have no idea what the specific problem was but it was serious enough to put up a barrier between them. Basically, they are not on speaking terms—period.

A stubborn farmer was ploughing his field. A neighbour watching him as he tried to guide the mule, finally said: 'I don't want to butt in but you could save yourself a lot of work by saying "heehaw" instead of jerking on the reins!' The old-timer mopped his brow and said: 'Yes, I know, but this here mule kicked me six years ago and I ain't spoke to him since!'

Up to this point Euodia and Syntyche had been the best of friends, they were in and out of each others home all the time. It was a real humdinger whatever happened. Now they cannot stand the sight of each other.

They may be adult in age and height, but they are awfully childish in their attitudes. Big children.

To add fuel to the fire, these women were not just happy-clappy pew warmers. They were actively involved in the work of God. They shared warm fellowship with Paul and were a colossal asset to him. Many times they worked cheek by jowl with each other and with him so as to ensure the furtherance of the gospel.

Paul says they *contended (synathleō) at my side in the cause of the gospel (euangelion), along with Clement (Klēmēs) and the rest (loipos) of my fellow workers (synergos), whose names (onoma) are in the book (biblos) of life (zōē).*

Irrespective of their track record, the enemy fired a poison dart that permeated their relationship. They clashed. Tempers flared. They boiled over. Words were said. Sparks flew. Result: two lives poles apart. And the ripples are such that it reaches beyond the small radius of their relationship. It spills over and adversely affects the whole church family to a greater or lesser degree. And two millennia down the road, that is all these women are remembered for.

The two of them have it in for each other. None will give a centimetre of ground. They stand on their own Bill of Rights. They stick to their guns. None is prepared to say: 'I'm sorry!'

They dig their stiletto heels in and walk around with a macro chip on their shoulder.

A grudge match

Here is a church which, in the goodness of God, was started by women and now it is being savaged and torn apart because of two headstrong women. They obviously were not living up to their names for Euodia means 'sweet fragrance' and Syntyche means 'affable'.

So disruptive was the controversy raging between them, it has been suggested that if the Philippians were Paul's crown, then Euodia and Syntyche were two thorns in that crown. I am tempted to rename them: Euodia to Odious and Syntyche to Soon Touchy.

Sad. Mature ladies acting like spoilt brats.

Without doubt, Paul passionately pleads with them to get their act together. He urges them, implores them, to patch up their differences and be good friends again. Paul, in his wisdom, does not take sides and blame one or the other. He has been around long enough to know it takes two to tango. There are always faults on both sides. As they say, there are three sides to every story—Euodia's side, Syntyche's side, and the truth.

Pique

The road that leads to a breakdown in harmony is never a one-way street—both of them are equally to blame for the hiatus in their relationship. Both are, therefore, responsible to see that it gets sorted out, one way or the other. Each must make the first move.

They need to get off their high horses and step down to reality. They need to back down for no one ever choked on swallowed pride. They need to sit down and talk again. They need to eat humble pie if they are to banish their feelings of resentment. They need to meet on a common piece of ground which Paul says is *in the Lord.*

Life is far too short to hold spite and get peeved with other people. They may not always see eye to eye with each other but they can still disagree without being disagreeable. With God's help, they can forgive each other and start over again. A dislocated member of the body is of little use to anyone. God wants them back in full fellowship and restored to their former usefulness. He wants to see them back in their proper place, not out of joint.

They are the ones who are losing out. They are missing out. Big time. As Charles Swindoll says: 'The peace and contentment and joy that could be theirs was draining away, like water down the drain of an unplugged bathtub.'

A go-between

Paul is realistic enough to know if they could not get together and sort the problem out between themselves then it may take someone to act as a conciliator-cum-facilitator. A third person may just be needed as a kind of arbitrator. This is the one Paul refers to as a *loyal (gnēsios) yokefellow (syzgos).* He would be a mediator or middleman. He would have the best interests of the entire church fellowship at heart so he would be an ideal go-between. His principal aim is reconciliation.

We have no way of knowing the outcome of this meeting of minds. For better or worse, the sequel has not been written. Time will tell. Eternity will reveal all. Hopefully, it will have been blessed with a measure of success.

The story is told of two porcupines who were huddled close together on a bitterly cold night up in northern Canada. The closer they got to stay warm, the more their quills pricked each other, making it virtually impossible for them to remain side by side. Silently they moved apart.

Before long they were shivering in the wintry gale, so they came back together again. Soon both were poking and jabbing each other ... so they separated again! Same story. Same result. Their action was repeated all night long—back and forth, back and forth.

Our two quarrelsome friends, Euodia and Syntyche, are just like the Canadian porcupines—they needed each other, but they kept needling each other. Point made.

4:4

Depressed mode

- Problem #1: the danger of losing ground.
- Problem #2: the danger of losing face.
- Problem #3: the danger of losing heart.

The Philippians were discouraged and disheartened. They opened the window of their lives and their joy has flown. Their smiles have gone. Their enthusiasm has dissipated. Their energy has waned. Their sense of excitement has all but evaporated. They are on a real downer. It is the whatever-day-of-the-week-it-is blues. They feel drained, exhausted, and harassed. They are running their lives on an empty tank. They show all the classic symptoms of the 'washed out and hanging out on the line to dry' syndrome. Agent blue.

Sure, there were many problems which impacted their lives from the outside, but perhaps the most distressing, damaging, and disturbing of all was the internal crisis—the festering sore of disunity among them. As is so often the case, they are the casualties caught up in the crossfire between the warring factions.

To these weary, pooped, bleary-eyed pilgrims, Paul writes a prescription that will lift their hearts and set them back—rejuvenated and reinvigorated—on the road to recovery. He says: *Rejoice in the Lord always. I will say it again: Rejoice!*

'Joy bubbles and brims at the heart of God, the heart of reality. God is an overflowing fountain of joy, a volcanic explosion of joy, a trillion burning suns of joy.' (Peter Kreeft)

Say it once, say it twice

Rejoice! He does not only say it once, he says it a second time. Rejoice! It is not an optional extra nor is it an elective in God's school. It is a command to be obeyed. Not just some of the time when we are in the mood to do it and we have that feel-good factor in our lives. But all of the time.

The problem is that some Christian's have a joy that is so deep, it rarely rises to the surface. The fervent evangelist Billy Sunday (1862-1935) was of the opinion: 'To see some people you would think that the essentials of orthodox Christianity is to have a face so long that you could eat oatmeal out of the end of a gas pipe!'

Vance Havner reckoned he had seen 'more cheerful faces on iodine bottles than on some Christians.' It never ceases to amaze me how many Christians walk around as if they were weaned on a dill pickle. As the old farmer said: 'What's down in the well comes up in the bucket!'

Paul reminds them that they should not let things get them down or allow people to rob them of their joy in Jesus. Their felicity is focused and centred on Christ. Happiness is entirely external, it is circumstantial. We have all seen the Charlie Brown cartoon that defines happiness as a warm puppy. But suppose there is no puppy. Well, then, there is no happiness.

Joy is internal, it does not hinge upon circumstances. And even when there is no puppy, even when life crashes around our feet, we can still experience an exuberant sense of joy within. Robert Schuller is singing from the same page for he writes that 'the good news is that the bad news can be turned into good news when [we] change our attitude.'

Humanly speaking, that is not easy to do. It goes against the grain. But our joy is in the Lord. It is not in our changing circumstances, nor is it in our fluctuating fortunes as life can sometimes be like the proverbial yo-yo. It is *in the Lord*. He remains constant. He is unchanging. We can be radiant and sparkle even though we may feel rotten and off colour inside—our joy is in Jesus, our joy is Jesus.

'A kettle is up to its neck in hot water, but it still sings.' (Anonymous)

Singing in the rain

When we have a renewed sense of joy in the Lord, we quickly bounce back to where we once were in our relationship with God. A bit like the Comeback Kid philosophy—no matter how deflated or down in the dumps we are, there is always a way back when we start praising the Lord for who he is. When the once silent chords begin to vibrate in our lives, they will prove to be a marvellous antidote to all our cares and concerns.

Such a *joie de vivre* is conspicuous, continuous, and contagious. It will be heard in our songs. It will be seen in the twinkle in our eyes. It will be recognised by the warm glow of our personalities. It will add an extra metre to our every footstep. We savour the taste of authentic joy in the flavourless tracks of everyday life and work. 'The Christian,' according to Augustine, 'should be an alleluia from head to foot.'

As the blind Scottish hymnwriter George Matheson (1842-1906) sang:

O Joy, that seekest me through pain,
I cannot close my heart to thee;
I trace the rainbow through the rain,
And feel the promise is not vain:
That morn shall tearless be.

Yes, people are problems. Big problems. That is why we need to:

- stand together (*cf.* 4:1),
- think together (*cf.* 4:2),
- work together (*cf.* 4:3), and
- praise together (*cf.* 4:4).

Whatever the problem, whoever the people, we can live a life of continual rejoicing. The best time to start is now.

4:5

Checkmate

Are you into chess? I came across a wonderful story recently that captured my imagination. In the early part of the nineteenth century an artist painted a picture of a chess game. The players were a young man and Satan. The young man manipulated the white pieces, Satan the black ones. If the young man were to win, he would be forever free from the power of evil—if Satan were to win, the young man would be his servant forever.

The artist, a great chess player himself, had the pieces lined up in such a way that the devil had just moved his queen and announced checkmate in four moves. The young man was seen hovering over his rook, his face pale with fear.

For years the picture hung in an art gallery with chess players from all over the world coming to ponder the configuration of the pieces, convinced that the devil had won. Yet one day a famous chess player named Paul Morphy was brought into the gallery to view the picture. He stood there, gesturing with his hands, as in his imagination he eliminated one move after another. To the amazement of all, the old man figured out a combination of moves that would defeat Satan.

'Young man, make that move!' he shouted.

Brave heart, big heart

Just when we think the devil has outplayed us, God reminds us that there is a move we can execute. The enemy may shout 'checkmate!' but God can show us a move we can make that has not crossed the enemy's mind.

And here it is in verses 5-9. It is a positive course of action that Paul advocates we take. He begins by breaking new ground when he says: *Let your gentleness (epeikēs) be evident (ginōskō) to all.* It is a most unusual word as I understand this is the only time it is used in the Greek New Testament. Some translations such as the KJV favour the term 'moderation'. It means 'forbearance' or 'sweet reasonableness'. A modern idiom would be 'easygoing'.

The kind of person Paul sees here is someone who is easy to get along with, in whose company we can relax and feel at home, who brings out the best in us. Someone generous in spirit, kind, and considerate—the genial sort of individual. Good-natured. Good-humoured. An amiable soul. Here is a cameo of a big-hearted Christian:

- they have a heart for God's people,
- they have a heart for lost people, and
- they have a heart for God.

Big-hearted! That is the secret to a life in touch and in tune with God. A heart that reaches up to heaven, that reaches down to those in need, that reaches out to those around us. What do big-hearted Christians have about them that causes us to sit up and take notice? In the next few verses Paul details four rich qualities reflected in their lives.

Enjoying God's presence

People of this calibre revel in the nearness of Jesus. They lap it up. Says Paul: *The Lord is near (engys)*. He is at hand. Close by. By faith, we can reach out and touch him. The old Quakers put it well when they said: 'the Lord is at your elbow.' Yes, he is as near as that. We luxuriate in his closeness.

There are many lonely people in today's world, many feel hemmed in, cut off, and isolated from their friends and family. They feel boxed in spending long tedious hours with their own company and their own thoughts. To all such, the Lord is near for joy is the echo of the presence of Christ in our lives.

In the best of times, the Lord is with us. In the worst of times, the Lord is still with us. In every changing circumstance of life, in all seasons of life, he is a friend at all times. He is not only present when the sun shines, he is there when the tempest rages and it blows a hurricane. The weather makes no difference to the Lord Jesus. He is there.

- The Lord stands up for us.

- The Lord stands with us.
- The Lord stands by us.

'Counting Jesus as never absent is holiness evermore.' (Hudson Taylor)

Many years ago under Stalin a group of thirty Russian peasants were meeting in secret for worship. Suddenly their service was interrupted by the arrival of the dreaded secret police. The leader ordered one of his men to take down the name of every assembled person. When this was done, an older man spoke up and said: 'There is one name you haven't got.' The officer snapped: 'I have them all.' The grey haired man replied: 'Believe me, there's one name you don't have.'

A recount was made, after which the officer said roughly: 'I told you I had them all. I have thirty names!' The aged saint again insisted there was one name he did not have on his list. At that point, the officer said: 'Who is it then? Speak out, who is it?' The old man, with a smile that matched his courage, said: 'The Lord Jesus Christ!'

4:6

Good psychology, God's psychology

Do not be anxious (merimnaō) about anything (mēdeis), but in everything (pas), by prayer (proseuchē) and petition (deēsis), with thanksgiving (eucharistia), present (gnōrizō) your requests (aitēma) to God. 'Why pray when you can worry' seems to be the slogan in vogue for many of God's people. Not unlike the man who quipped: 'I've got so many troubles right now that if anything bad happens today, it will be two weeks before I can worry about it.'

The person Paul thinks about here is someone who taps the humongous potential of heaven. They explore the possibilities open to them as they storm the gates of glory. Instead of listening to hearsay, they prove for themselves that God hears and answers prayer. The big-hearted Christian, therefore, takes his whopping burdens to the Lord and leaves them there. He knows that life is fragile so he handles it with prayer.

In our experience, how often do we come before the Lord with our nagging worries and, after a few minutes of heartfelt prayer, get up from our knees, pick up our haversack of cares and walk away with them again? Sound familiar. Probably. Says Paul, why worry when you can pray. Worry looks around, faith looks up.

> *It's not the work but the worry*
> *That makes the world grow old,*
> *That numbers the years of its children*
> *Ere half their story is told,*
> *That weakens their faith in heaven*
> *And the wisdom of God's great plan,*
> *It's not the work but the worry*
> *That breaks the heart of man.*

Passing the buck

Joe was a perpetual worrier that his friends labelled him as such. One day Bill was walking down the Main Street when he saw something that really amazed him. Joe was on the far side of the road and whistling away. Bill could hardly believe his eyes and ears.

When he crossed over and spoke with Joe, he asked him outright: 'Joe, what on earth has happened to you? I've never seen a happier man!'

He said: 'It's great, Bill, I haven't worried now for several weeks.'

'That's super, Joe. How did you manage it?' enquired Bill.

'Well,' said Joe, 'it was dead easy! I've hired a man to do all the worrying for me!'

'What?' gasped Bill. 'You've hired a man to do it for you! I've never heard of anyone doing that before. How much does he charge you?'

'A thousand dollars a week,' said Joe, with a smile on his face.

'That's a lot of money! How could you possibly raise a thousand bucks a week to pay him?' wondered Bill out loud.

'That's his worry!' replied Joe.

A modern beatitude states: 'Blessed is the person who is too busy in the day to worry and too tired at night to do it.'

Hurry, worry, bury

We derive our English word 'worry' from the German word 'wurgen' which means 'to strangle or choke'. Our Lord used the same word picture on one occasion when he related the story of the sower, the seed, and the soils (*cf.* Mark 4:14-19). That is what worry does—it cuts off our lifeline and blocks the airways in our lives. We feel as if someone has tied a ligature around our necks. Crushingly effective. Devastatingly potent. Needless to say, the consequences are alarmingly serious.

Spiritually, worry assaults our faith and we end up in a fog of doubt that blurs the face of God and muffles the voice of God. Physically, it steals our health for many of the medical problems that ravage our bodies are either stress induced or stress related. Emotionally, it destroys our peace and sense of well-being for the serenity necessary for a normal life evaporates and vanishes into thin air. Mark Twain made the valid observation: 'I am an old man and have known many troubles, but most of them never happened.'

When travelling recently in the American state of Georgia, I noticed a wayside pulpit in front of an old country church that said: 'Worry is when we pay the interest on trouble before the bill comes due!'

Such is worry—it pulls tomorrow's clouds over today's sunshine. The Carolinian preacher, Vance Havner, is on record as saying that 'worry is like a rocking chair—it will give you something to do but it won't get you anywhere!'

Alternatives to worry

Paul makes it clear that we should worry about nothing and pray about everything. Pray is a four-letter word that we can say anywhere. It should be top priority rather than seen as a last resort, something we do when all else fails. We are to stop fumbling with our worry beads and begin sharing our concerns with Jesus. He wants to do the worrying for us. And when we offload them on to his shoulders, anxiety will drain from our hearts like water from a sieve.

Billy Graham's wife Ruth often tells the story of the weary Christian who lay awake at night trying to hold the world together by his worrying. One night he heard the Lord gently say to him: 'Now you go to sleep, Jim. I'll sit up! There's no point in the two of us staying awake all night!'

Joseph Medicott Scriven (1819-86) understood, perhaps more than most, what Paul was talking about when he wrote:

What a friend we have in Jesus,
All our sins and griefs to bear!
What a privilege to carry
Everything to God in prayer.
O what peace we often forfeit,
O what needless pain we bear,
All because we do not carry
Everything to God in prayer!

We need to download our worries and get online with God.

Everything means everything. The big things in life as well as the small insignificant issues. I go along with Jerry Vines when he writes that 'nothing is too big for God's greatness and nothing is too small for God's care.' No matter what it is, God wants to hear about it. He really is interested. If it affects you, it greatly concerns him.

Why should we deprive him of the privilege of sharing with us in our tension-packed moments? The way to ward off worry is to switch our needs from our worry list to our prayer list, because God answers knee-mail. Paul tells us how to do it.

By prayer—this is when we bring our many requests to the throne of grace. It carries with it the idea of adoration, devotion, and worship. It is when we see the greatness and grandeur of God, when we come face to face with his awesome majesty and we sense in our spirits that he is bigger than all our problems.

A day hemmed in prayer is less likely to unravel.

And petition—this is supplication which is an earnest seeking after God. It is sincere. It is spiritual conflict and highlights the intensity of our praying. An example of such an encounter is where Christ prayed all alone, under the gnarled olive trees, in the Garden of Gethsemane (*cf.* Luke 22:39-44). It is urgent, specific, and particular prayer. It is not going around the world for a shortcut, it is straight to the point.

Thanksgiving—is to be mingled often with our asking. This is when we have a profound sense of appreciation for who God is and for all that he has done for us. Our prayer is to be accompanied with a spirit of gratitude—gratitude fills. Praise springs from an awareness of the abundant goodness and many mercies of God.

A bright and cheery old lady in a testimony meeting said: 'You know, dears, there's always something for us to be thankful for. I only have two teeth but, thank God, they both meet!'

- Be careful for nothing!
- Be prayerful for everything!
- Be thankful for anything!

In this context, the words of Elizabeth Cheney's poem spring to mind:

Said a robin to a sparrow:
'I should really like to know
Why these anxious human beings
Rush around and worry so.'

Said the sparrow to the robin:
'I suppose that it must be
That they have no heavenly Father
Such as cares for you and me!'

'Relax. I'm in control.' GOD

4:7

Shalom

Paul speaks here about something which all of us want but few of us have—peace.

- Peace with God.
- Peace with ourselves.
- Peace with our partner.
- Peace with our friends and colleagues.
- Peace with our past, our present, and our future.

This peace is not a spiritual marshmallow, full of softness and sweetness but without much actual substance.

It is surprisingly full of strength and vigour. Peace! The undisturbableness of God reigning in our lives. It is far more wonderful than the human mind can understand. It is incomprehensible, surpassing our wildest dreams. A Scotsman would say that 'it is better felt than telt!'

When we stop worrying and start praying then we experience his peace in our hearts and minds. Away with all our fears. Banish every care. We wave them farewell and, as we do, we receive the peace of God. Welcome relief.

And the peace (eirēnē) of God, which transcends (hyperechō) all understanding (nous), will guard (phroureō) your hearts (kardia) and your minds (noēma) in Christ Jesus. The apostle sees God's peace as a garrison for the heart and a guard for the mind. It is something to be experienced today in the hour of trial or triumph, in moments of pain or pleasure, in seasons of sorrow or joy. This is the peace of Galilee in storm and Gethsemane in crisis.

This peace is a sentinel at the door of the heart and mind, all day, all night, all year. 24/7/365. When Satan would attempt to attack us and invade our lives then the sentry is on duty. Colonel Peace is standing guard. He keeps constant watch and deters any intruder from a forced entry. He is a kind of spiritual surveillance system to monitor our hearts. Thank God, he never fails.

It is a quiet confidence in him, a relaxing in his love, a resting in his caring arms—an inner composure which only comes when we are fully trusting in him. The storm may be hurricane force on the outside but we have a deep calm on the inside. It is designed for the heart as it protects us from wrong feelings. And it is tailor-made for the mind to protect us from wrong thinking. In the words of Isaiah, it is 'perfect peace' (Isaiah 26:3).

John Wesley, the Methodist revivalist preacher, said: 'When I looked to Jesus, the dove of peace flew into my heart—when I looked at the dove of peace, it flew away!' It seems to me that God not only wants us to rest in peace after we die, he wants us to rest in peace before we die.

4:8

God chasers

Paul reminds us in this verse to think with a clear mind and a clean mind. You are not what you think you are, but what you think, you are. True. That puts the ball back into our court—we may not be able to select our circumstances but we can choose our attitude.

Here is a menu for the mind. It we follow these guidelines then we will continue to win the war over worry. Thinking right and right thinking fit hand in glove. He says: *Finally, brothers ... think (logizomai) about such things.*

We are to think about that which is genuine and sincere—*whatever is true (alēthēs).* We are to focus our minds on facts in preference to that which is deceptive or illusory. This is not fantasy or imagination run riot. We should not live in a dream world of make-believe but in the real world of holding on to that which is reliable.

The simplest way to expose a crooked line is to place a straight edge alongside it. A ship was threading its way through inshore islands when a lady asked the captain if he knew where all the rocks and shoals were. 'No Madam,' he replied, 'but I know where the deep water is.'

Whatever is noble (semnos)—this is no pat-on-the-head salesman's spiel. It is that which is honourable and above-board. It is something which is worthy of reverence because it has the dignity of holiness stamped upon it. Honesty is not the best policy for the Christian. In this context, it is the only one.

Whatever is right (dikaios)—that which is upright, just, and fair. It is a conversation or train of thought of which God would approve. It will have no time to think about rumours, or malicious scandal, or idle juicy gossip.

I agree with Adrian Rogers when he says that 'gossip is a form of insanity.' Have you ever met a gossip who knew they were a gossip? They say: 'You know me, I don't gossip.' And then they start to gossip! Well, if a person is doing something and they do not know they are doing it, I think they must have rooms to rent upstairs unfurnished. If it is wrong, it cannot be right.

Whatever is pure (hagnos)—in a murky world we should seek to be above and beyond reproach in our thought lives. A wholesome and healthy outlook is envisaged in this phrase. In an age when anything passes as acceptable we need to guard our minds from harbouring such filth and dirt. We should not allow our minds to dwell on that which is smutty, shabby, or soiled, lest we become defiled.

Whatever is lovely (prosphilēs)—this reminds us of those things which are amiable, pleasing, and agreeable. It is that which is commendable and beautiful. It is attractive and catches the eye and in so doing brings honour and glory to the name of Jesus. It is pleasing.

Whatever is admirable (euphēmos)—the encouragement here is to fix our minds on those things which are of outstandingly good report. They are virtuous. It is the epitome of graciousness and stands in stark contrast to the that's-just-me-and-people-can-take-it-or-leave-it mindset so prevalent in today's world.

An amazing list. But Paul is not finished yet. He picks up all six suggestions and places them in one basket with the proviso: *if anything is excellent (aretē) or praiseworthy (epainos)* think about it. If it is *excellent*, it will motivate and stimulate us to do better, and if it is *praiseworthy*, it is worth commending to others.

Go for quality every time. It is all in the mind. When it comes to your thought life and mine, how we think is important—about ourselves, others, and God.

The outstanding nineteenth-century preacher C H Spurgeon wrote: 'God will not live in the parlour of our hearts if we entertain the devil in the cellar of our thoughts.'

The story is told of an Englishman who wanted to know an American's secret for getting ahead in business. 'I'll tell you,' said the affable American. 'You should eat more fish. Fish is brain food. Give me five dollars and I'll get you some fish my wife fixes for me. Eat it and see how you get on.'

The impressed Englishman handed over the five dollars and the fish was duly delivered. The next day, when they met, the New Yorker asked whether any improvement had been noted. 'Well, no,' said the frustrated Englishman. 'But, tell me, isn't five dollars a bit high for such a small piece of fish?' The American was amused and beamed: 'There, now! Already your brain is beginning to work!'

My question is: what are you thinking about?

4:9

Sermon on Sunday, Saint on Monday

Paul says you have seen me, heard me, received from me, learned from me, now go out and live for God—*whatever you have learned (manthanō) or received (paralambanō) or heard (akouō) from me, or seen (horaō) in me—put it into practice (prassō)*. It is putting into practice what we have been taught. It is all about learning and living the Christian life. It is doing what God asks us to do and being what God wants us to be. It is not all theory. It works in the real world.

We do not want to be like the preacher of whom it was said: 'He preached so well in the pulpit that it was a tragedy for him ever to go out of it, but he lived so poorly at home that is was unfortunate he ever entered it.'

One Sunday on their way home from church, a little girl turned and said to her mother: *'Mum, the preacher's sermon this morning confused me.'* When her mother asked her to tell her what bothered her, the youngster said: *'Well, he said that God is bigger than we are. Is that true?'* *'Yes,'* said the mother, *'that is true.'* *'And he also said that God lives in us. Is that true?'* *'Yes, darling, that is true.'* *'Well,'* said the wide-eyed kid, *'if God is bigger than us and he lives in us, wouldn't he show through?'*

Paul's parting shot reminds us of the priceless bonus given to all those who are not held captive by the chains of tension or preoccupied with worry. This is the promise God makes to those who have moved on from the 'today is the tomorrow you worried about yesterday' attitude to living one day at a time.

He declares that the *God (Theos) of peace (eirēnē) will be with you.* Yes, we have peace with God, but we also have the God of peace. When we pray right, think right, and live right, then we have the sweet assurance of the presence of God with us. We will know the companionship of the God of peace and, as an added compensation, we will know the influence of the peace of God.

The last time I preached in Stornoway on the Isle of Lewis, my friend Ernie Garden shared with me a quote from Paul Rees on this relationship. He said: 'In verse 7 we had "the peace of God" for our guarding; here we have "the God of peace" for our going. And the second is even greater than the first!'

4:10, 11

Secret of contentment

In a cemetery somewhere in rural England there is a grave marker with the inscription: 'She died from want of things.' Adjacent to that marker is another which reads: 'He died trying to give them to her.'

My Oxford dictionary defines contentment as 'a satisfied state'. Sounds good. The only drawback is that it appears quite elusive. Almost impalpable. So many are looking for it but end up drawing a blank cheque. They are searching for it but never seem to find it. Their insatiable appetite leads them on one wild goose chase after another, but all they catch is a cold. So many people are discovering today that if something has a price tag attached to it then contentment seems even more distant. The fact is, until we make peace with who we are, we will never be content with what we have.

In his book, *Simple Faith*, Charles Swindoll cites a poem by Jason Lehman which expresses the discontent so prevalent in our 'I want more' society:

It was spring,
But it was summer I wanted.
The warm days,
And the great outdoors.

It was summer,
But it was autumn I wanted.
The colourful leaves,
And the cool, dry air.

It was autumn,
But it was winter I wanted.
The beautiful snow,
And the joy of the holiday season.

It was winter,
But it was spring I wanted.
The warmth
And the blossoming of nature.

I was a child,
But it was adulthood I wanted.
The freedom,
And the respect.

I was 20,
But it was 30 I wanted.
To be mature,
And sophisticated.

I was middle aged,
But it was 20 I wanted.
The youth,
And the free spirit.

I was retired,
But it was middle age I wanted.
The presence of mind,
Without limitations.

My life was over.
But I never got what I wanted.

What an awful way to live. What a sad way to go. Not satisfied. Not content. That is what happens when dreams become nightmares and when, like the proverbial dog, we bark up the wrong trees.

William Shakespeare in *King Henry VI* makes the point: 'My crown is in my heart not on my head; ... my crown call'd content; a crown it is that seldom kings enjoy.'

Paul found the secret—not in things, not in additives, not in anything. He discovered blissful contentment in Jesus Christ. Contentment can never be found in a safe-deposit box. It can be found only in the Lord. When a Christian reduces life to its lowest terms, it is Christ. He is the kernel. Everything else is husk. He alone is the basis for real contentment.

We can see this working out in Paul's life in the final verses of his upbeat letter to the Philippian believers. There he says: *I am not saying this because I am in need (hysterēsis), for I have learned (manthanō) to be content (autarkēs) whatever the circumstances.* How refreshingly honest.

It did not matter to him if it was hot or cold, wet or dry, or if he was free or fettered, inside or outside, he was plainly contented. No matter why! No matter what! No matter where! When we stop and think about it, that is what makes the difference between him and so many of us.

Thermo Christians

There are two types of Christians in the church of Christ—we are either thermometers or thermostats.

- A *thermometer* Christian is someone who merely registers what is around him. He does not change anything. He just records the prevailing temperature and it is always going up and down.
- A *thermostat* Christian is a person who regulates the atmosphere. They are agents for change and will not be affected by the direction the wind is blowing. They determine policy rather than let the situation dictate to them.

Paul is similar to a thermostat—spiritually, he was not up and down. He was not adversely influenced by the things that happened to him. He had a goal in life. He had a mission. He had a clearly defined objective. In every situation, he longed for Christ to be magnified.

He would change it before it changed him. That is the kind of man we have here—someone who influenced others for good. A catalyst. He precipitated change.

Why was he able to act in such a positive manner? He had the security of contentment in his own life. He never saw himself as a victim of his circumstances. He was a victor over them. A man can only do that when his heart is in the right place. He was relaxed—a man at ease with himself rather than someone sweating on the treadmill of self-improvement.

This was not a state of euphoria that he happened to fall into overnight, nor was it an indifferent could care less attitude. It was something he learned in the school of life. It is a gradual and progressive experience as one learns to cope with the rough as well as the smooth.

Paul had more than his fair share of problems, enough to give any man stage fright, but he came through in the end with a smile on his face and a story to tell to his followers. How? He developed the ability to accept the situation as it was and he adapted to it. For him, 'problems were only opportunities in work clothes' (Henry Kaiser). That is the road to contentment.

If only ...

Contentment actually means 'containment'. It is a most unusual expression but it has the idea of someone who is self-contained. His resources were on the inside and not dependent on substitutes from the outside. A self-sufficient person.

According to Paul's testimony it portrays a man who is at peace in Christ's sufficiency. It is when we believe that God is in total overall control. Because he lives within us and his genius and power is available to us, it means we can face all the demands and pressures of this life. We can cope through Jesus Christ. Our sufficiency is in him.

So many people go through life thinking that if they could only pack their bags and move upmarket to a new house in a leafy suburb, they would be content. If they could just go to another church which caters for all their needs and those of their family, they would be content. If they could get a new job with better prospects and have the opportunity to make a fresh start, they would be content.

'Discontent dislocates and disjoints the soul, it pulls off the wheels,' advises Thomas Watson in *The Art of Divine Contentment*. 'It is a fretting humour, which dries the brains, wastes the spirits, corrodes and eats out the comfort of life.'

'Christian contentment,' counters the Puritan Jeremiah Burroughs in *The Rare Jewel of Christian Contentment*, 'is that sweet, inward, quiet, gracious frame of spirit, which freely submits to and delights in God's wise and fatherly disposal in every condition.'

Excess baggage

Apparently a man came to the Greek philosopher Socrates (469-399 BC) on one occasion and asked him about the unhappiness of one of their mutual friends.

Socrates answered: *'The trouble with that man is that he takes himself with him wherever he goes.'*

We all do! Having said that, there were a number of factors that contributed to Paul's idyllic feeling of blessed contentment. He was always on the move from A to B and was daily confronted with new challenges and opportunities. Sure. Through it all, however, I see a man who is not stressed-out and swallowing prescription drugs by the handful, but a man who is the epitome of contentment—simply satisfied. Satisfied with Jesus. James McGranahan (1840-1907) says it all:

O Christ, in thee my soul hath found,
And found in thee alone,
The peace, the joy I sought so long,
The bliss till now unknown.

Now none but Christ can satisfy,
None other name for me!
There's love, and life, and lasting joy,
Lord Jesus, found in thee.

Shirt free

The story is told of a king who suffered from a particularly painful ailment. He went to an advisor who told him the only cure was for him to find a contented man, ask for his shirt, and then wear it night and day. The king immediately despatched messengers throughout his realm to seek out just such a man and to bring back his shirt.

Months passed and after a thorough search of the kingdom the messengers returned—empty-handed.

'Do you mean to tell me that you could not find a single contented man in all my realm?' the king asked indignantly.

'O sire,' the messengers replied, 'we found such a man, but only one in all thy realm.'

'Then why did you not bring back his shirt for me?' the king demanded.

'Master, the man *had* no shirt,' they answered.

Shirt or no shirt, a person with a positive, clear-cut faith in God is content. Always.

Belief in the providence of God

I rejoice greatly in the Lord that at last you have renewed (anathallō) *your concern (phroneō) for me. Indeed, you have been concerned, but* *you had no opportunity (akaireomai) to show it.* One writer makes this fairly ordinary verse come alive with his colourful comments. He says: 'Who is saying this? Some young turk who has just turned the deal on his first million? A superstar who recently signed an unbelievable contract? Some guy in his twenties about to set sail on a magnificent adventure?

Not on your life. Would you believe, a sixty-plus year old Jew chained to a Roman guard under house arrest, not knowing if tomorrow he will be killed, brought to court, or set free?

'Though getting up in years, he is rejoicing. Though without the comforts of home and the privileges of privacy, he is happy. Though he does not have a clue regarding his future, he is smiling at life. Though he is set aside, forced to stay in one place, completely removed from the excitement of a broader ministry, he is still rejoicing. No matter what happened to him, Paul refused to be caught in the grip of pessimism.'

When Paul reflects on his personal situation and it dawns upon him that the church at Philippi had shown a measure of love and concern for him just when he needed it most, he put it all down to the perfect timing of God. Providence. That is what we call it even though we cannot adequately explain it. We only know that God is working on our behalf and he orders events so that everything fits perfectly into place. It is the unseen hand of God guiding the hearts of men.

Jottings on Joseph

The story of Joseph is a superb illustration of such a truth. His brothers sold him off as a slave. Pride, envy, and jealousy got the better of them. The day came, however, when Joseph and his brothers met face to face. When he revealed himself to them, he knew that they would be afraid of him.

But Joseph surprised them by looking at his fate from a divine perspective. He told them that they should not be grieved because of what happened for God used these events to preserve the lives of tens of thousands of people through the preparation that Egypt made for the present famine. Then he summarised his attitude in one cryptic statement: 'So then, it was not you who sent me here, but God' (Genesis 45:8).

The theology of Joseph can be summed up in two phrases—'you sold me' but 'God sent me' (Genesis 45:5, 8). He understood that behind the perverse hand of his brothers was the purposeful hand of God. A God who sees events before they happen. A God who sees the future with precise clarity because he is the one who works events according to his perfect plan. Even while things appear to be out of hand or off-course,

God is there working invisibly behind the scenes (*cf.* Ecclesiastes 7:13, 14).

Behind a frowning providence, God's face is smiling.

No matter what takes place in our lives, as Paul found to his personal pleasure, we can rest in the fact that God is behind the scenes directing the scenes he is behind. It is absolutely thrilling to realise that behind each scene we can see the shadow of the Almighty directing from the wings. All the ups and downs of life bear God's autograph.

Warren Wiersbe reminds us that 'life is not a series of accidents but a series of appointments.' So far as the child of God is concerned, it is not chance or coincidence. It is not hit-and-run or even hit-and-miss. It is certainly not the luck of the draw or picking the shortest straw. No fluke. No big break. Thank God! The abiding principle is enshrined in the unforgettable words of Mordecai: 'And who knows but that you have come to royal position for such a time as this' (Esther 4:14).

4:12

In the right place

Paul was not living in cloud-cuckoo-land as he related his own experience of the contented life. For him the rubber was hitting the road. At times it may have been a bumpy ride but it was always blessed. Not utopian, but thoroughly enjoyable.

Let him speak for himself: *I know (oida) what it is to be in need (tapeinoō), and I know what it is to have plenty (perisseuō). I have learned the secret (myeō) of being content in any and every situation, whether well fed (chortazō) or hungry (peinaō), whether living in plenty or in want (hystereō).*

According to one source, there are four basic things for the believer to be concerned about:

- What I put on—clothes.
- What I put in—food.

- What I put up—a house to live in.
- What I put away—money for the future.

Paul Rees tells the anecdote that years ago a syndicated column carried the story of a group of famous American financiers who in the early 1920s met at the Edgewater Beach Hotel in Chicago. In personal wealth and financial clout, they controlled more money than was in the national treasury. From time to time, their names appeared in the press, their influence was enormous, their success fabulous. Legendary.

Twenty-five years later the same columnist called the roll of these princes of the financial world. One of them, a man who cornered millions through wheat speculation, died abroad, insolvent. Another, the president of the nation's largest independent steel company, died penniless. The president of the New York Stock Exchange had recently been released from prison. A member of the Cabinet in the Harding administration, after being let out of prison for health reasons, died at home. The greatest exploiter of the Bear market in Wall Street committed suicide. The leader of the world's greatest monopoly died at his own hand. In summarising the list of men, the writer with remarkable perception noted that 'all of these men had learned how to make big money, but not one of them had learned how to live.'

What a radical difference in the life of Paul. He had learned to live. When he could not see the bright side, he polished the dull side. God never failed him, he never let him down—not once!

Yes, there were times when the going was tough out there as he ran into the wind and there were other times when the sun shone in his face; there were days of poverty and there were days of plenty; there were days when money was scarce and there were better times when he had so much he did not know what to do with it; there were meal times when he had to go without and feel the gnawing pangs of hunger and there were other occasions when he sat down to a five-course feast à la carte.

Clark Poling, a US Army chaplain in the Second World War, gave his lifebelt to drowning soldiers when their troopship, *The Dorchester*, was torpedoed. Before leaving on his last voyage, Poling had written home to his parents: 'I know I shall have your prayers; but please, don't pray simply that God will keep me safe. War is a dangerous business. Pray that God will make me adequate.' God did.

And Paul would have applauded for, like Poling, he was where God wanted him to be. In the right place, at the right time, that is the cue for contentment.

4:13

Ready for anything ... RFA

This is the ideal motto text for every Christian—*I can do (ischyō) everything through him who gives me strength (endynamoō)*. We would be hard-pressed to find a better watchword for our daily lives. It is not a matter of hangin' in there or holdin' on tighter. It is a vote of confidence in the know-how and ability of Jesus.

Richard A. Swenson in his book *Margin* reminds us that 'God did not intend this verse to represent a negation of life balance.' Jesus did not heal all, he did not minister to all, he did not visit all, and he did not teach all. He did not work twenty-four-hour ministry days.

The problem with so many of our lives is that when God calls, he gets the busy signal.

When it comes to any kind of ministry and the pressures associated with it, we cannot do it on our own but through Christ we can do it. It means we are continually energised in all things by the strengthening of Christ. He is the one who empowers us so that we are able to operate at maximum efficiency.

That means when our knees are knocking and our legs feel like jelly, when the butterflies are in the stomach, when we break out in a cold sweat, we can still do whatever task is assigned to us because of the enabling of Jesus.

This is the quintessence of Christian living. We can be ready for anything. And with his strength infused within us, we are able for everything. He not only gives us the power to live, he is the power for living. To know the conscious and continual power of the indwelling Christ guarantees the strength to live:

- faithfully (*cf.* 4:1),
- joyfully (*cf.* 4:4),
- helpfully (*cf.* 4:5),
- prayerfully (*cf.* 4:6a),
- thankfully (*cf.* 4:6b),
- peacefully (*cf.* 4:7), and
- thoughtfully (*cf.* 4:8).

4:14-18

He knew the right people

Paul knows how to motivate people and he does it wonderfully well. He is one of the finest examples of man management that we read of anywhere. We only have to read what he says to them about their care and concern for him. He does not flatter or sweet-talk them. He sincerely thanks them. This epistle is, among other things, a letter of receipt, an acknowledgment of their many love gifts.

Yet it was good (kalōs) of you to share (synkoinōneō) in my troubles (thlipsis). Moreover, as you Philippians know, in the early (archē) days of your acquaintance with the gospel, when I set out (exerchomai) from Macedonia (Makedonia), not one church (ekklēsia) shared (koinōneō) with me in the matter of giving (dosis) and receiving (lēmpsis), except you only; for even when I was in Thessalonica (Thessalonikē), you sent me aid again and again when I was in need (chreia). Not that I am looking (epizēteō) for a gift (doma), but I am looking for what may be credited (pleonazō) to your account (logos). I have received full payment (apechō) and even more; I am amply supplied (plēroō), now that I have received from Epaphroditus the gifts you sent. They are a fragrant (osmē) offering (thysia), an acceptable (dektos) sacrifice, pleasing (euarestos) to God.

It is obvious from what Paul says that these folks were loyal to the core in their regular support of the apostle. They were not embarrassed when he found himself in big trouble and was tossed unceremoniously into prison. They kept on giving. It would appear from reading between the lines that there were, in the early days, no other local churches involved in his maintenance.

The Philippian assembly seemed to carry the load themselves, and they did so with a heart and a half. And even when he was ministering in another church they continued to send him assurances of their love. Here was a local church that gave generously and liberally to the Lord's work through his servant and they prospered spiritually as a result of such noble endeavour.

Charles Swindoll aptly comments: 'They never second guessed the apostle in his decision to move on, they supported him. They neither judged him when things went well nor complained when times were hard and he had no fruit to show for his labour, they supported him. They felt pain when he hurt, they prayed for him when he was unable to stay in touch, and they sent friends to comfort him when he was in prison. What a church! No wonder Paul felt such affection for them.'

He just wants them to know how much he is indebted to them for their practical fellowship—that is what makes this the most famous 'thank you' note in history. Through them, all his needs have been met and all the bills paid. And there was even some left over for a rainy day (*cf.* 4:18). Paul is most appreciative of their sacrificial support, prayerfully, financially, every way. He likens their giving to a budding tree in verse 10, and to an investment in verses 14-17.

It is compared in verse 18 to a fragrant offering with which God is well pleased. A closer examination reinforces the truth that the person who is in receipt of the gift is singularly blessed, and the people who give the gift are doubly blessed. And, in a new dimension to giving, God is blessed.

4:19

Standing on the promises of God

It was Hudson Taylor (1832-1905), founder in 1865 of the former China Inland Mission (OMF International), who coined the phrase: 'When God's work is done in God's way for God's glory, it will not lack God's supply.' This is the verse he staked his faith on—a verse I learned at my mother's knee: *And my God will meet (plēroō) all your needs (chreia) according to (kata) his glorious (doxa) riches (ploutos) in Christ Jesus.*

The friends at Philippi dug deeply into their pockets to meet Paul's needs, in return they could expect God to look after their many needs. Not their wants, but their needs! I agree with Zig Zaglar that 'life is an echo. What you send out—you get back. What you give—you get.' The lesson is: do not be afraid of giving. It is the first step to receiving.

God's shovel is bigger than theirs!

The Lord would recompense them and they would prove that those who give to God will always have something to give. Their supplies might be running low but they would never run out. The Philippians gave out of their meagre resources but God gives to them according to his inexhaustible wealth. Look at it like this:

- it was personal—*my God,*
- it was positive—*will meet,*
- it was pointed—*all your needs,*
- it was plentiful—*according to his glorious riches,* and
- it was powerful—*in Christ Jesus.*

Eugene Peterson paraphrases it wonderfully well: 'You can be sure that God will take care of everything you need, his generosity exceeding even yours in the glory that pours from Jesus' (*The Message*).

C H Spurgeon referred to this verse as 'the cheque book of the bank of faith.' We write in the amount we need, God fills in the rest and then signs his name on the dotted line. It never bounces. It is always enough for God gives on a scale worthy of his wealth.

A dear old lady lived all alone in a downtown apartment in upstate New York. She was a widow and a devout Christian. Her landlord was a convinced atheist. All the time he would laugh at her and mock her because of her simple faith in Jesus Christ.

One day he walked by her apartment and he noticed the door was slightly ajar. He stopped in his tracks for he heard her talking to someone— she was praying—praying for food as the cupboard was empty, there was nothing on the shelves and her pension had been used to pay some unexpected bills. She was claiming the promise in verse 19.

The atheist decided when she went out that he would play a joke on her. He purchased three bags of groceries with plenty of meat, fruit, and veg and left them on the table in her kitchen. And then he hid behind the door waiting for her to come back. When she returned, she saw the food on the table, and the first thing she did was thank the Lord for his unfailing goodness and faithfulness to her.

That was more than the atheist could swallow. He jumped out from behind the door and told her he had bought them and it had nothing to do with God! The saintly lady looked at him and said: 'O, that's all right with me. God gave these groceries to me even if he sent them by the devil!'

4:20

Glory to God

To our God and Father be glory for ever (aiōn) and ever. Amen (amēn). When we invest our lives and our resources in the kingdom of God then he gets the corresponding glory. He deserves it. He is worthy of it. It is rightfully his. It belongs to him. It is not only for the measurable years of time, but for a measureless eternity. The glory will always be ascribed to him. And that is the way it must be.

'When we bless God for mercies, we prolong them. When we bless God for miseries, we end them. Praise is the honey of life which a devout heart extracts from every bloom of providence and grace.' (C H Spurgeon)

4:21, 22

Greetings to them

Paul rounds the chapter off with a marvellous series of greetings when he writes: *Greet (aspazomai) all the saints (hagios) in Christ Jesus. The brothers (adelphos) who are with me send greetings. All the saints send you greetings, especially (malista) those who belong to Caesar's (Kaisar) household (oikia).*

This is fantastic as it underlines the affinity we share in the family of God. There are three groups of people referred to. The first group who are with him would probably have included men like Timothy, Dr Luke, Epaphroditus, Aristarchus from Thessalonica, Tychicus from Asia, and maybe Epaphras the evangelist from Colossae.

The second group is believed by many to be those whose names are listed in Romans 16. Among them are Ampliatus, Apelles, Stachys, Rufus, Hermes, Tryphena, and Tryphosa. Many of them are relatively unknown to us but each one would be known to those in Philippi.

The final group is the one that has caused most interest over the years. To whom is he referring? Who is included? Could he have in mind the emperor's wife and children bearing in mind that legend has it that, while Nero was out of town, his wife listened to the Christian message and turned her life over to Jesus Christ?

The description surely refers to an incredibly large number of people from all over the empire. Since 'all roads lead to Rome' it would have included slaves, soldiers, senators, men and women of wealth and status, and many others who were drawn to the city and its environs because it was the nerve centre for the expanding empire. There would be those members of the elite Imperial Guard who waited on Caesar doing his special work. And there would also be those who worked in the corridors of power doing all sorts of jobs.

What thrills me more than anything else is that Christ has invaded and infiltrated the very citadel of unbelief. In the very rooms where his name had been an unmentionable, Christ as Lord was now being openly discussed. The inaugural meeting of the Workers Christian Fellowship was probably held there and then. And all of this was happening right under Nero's nose, yet he could not stop it! It blows the mind. That is why we give God all the glory. Yet again, he has brought about an unbelievable ending from an uneventful beginning.

4:23

Grace for you

The grace (charis) of the Lord Jesus Christ be with your spirit (pneuma). Amen. Thus Paul began his letter in 1:2, thus Paul ended it in 4:23. The focus in every verse, if not every line, has been on Jesus. He is grace personified. Or, in the timely words of J A Motyer: 'Grace is Jesus being gracious.'

It is God's unmerited, unlimited favour that shines upon us all the time along all the way. Grace upon grace! Grace that makes us ready for anything and grace that means we lack for nothing. It was grace that set our feet on the highway to heaven. It is grace that keeps us company all the journey through. It is grace that will see us safely home at last.

What a marvellous way to end a letter. *Amen* is what he says. And so say all of us.

Paul has nothing more to say. He rolls up the scroll and gives it to his friend Epaphroditus. They pray together. Paul bids him a fond farewell as he knows their paths will never cross again this side of heaven. He journeyed home to Philippi with the letter stuffed in his back pocket.

When he arrived, he gathered the church together and they heard what Paul had to say for the first time. They read it again, and again, and again. They got the message! Have you?

Study Guide

~ compiled by John White ~

Chapter One

1. Why does Paul call the Philippians *saints* in verse 1, and what are the implications of this description for you and me?

2. What can we learn about 'doing church' from verse 1?

3. How were the Philippians *partners in the gospel* with Paul in verse 5, and how do you think this made Paul feel? What is the primary lesson for us here?

4. What is the *good work* that is mentioned in verse 6? Do you share Paul's confidence of inevitable progress in your own life, and what difference can this confidence make to our lives today?

5. What do you understand in verse 6 by the phrase *the day of Christ Jesus*? How does your comprehension affect the way that you live (if at all!)?

6. If someone who was going through a hard time in their life came to you for help, what could you share with them from verses 12-14 that might encourage them?

7. Sometimes one of the most difficult things for us to deal with is when we are hurt by other Christians. What do verses 15-18 show us about some of the right ways to respond when this happens?

8. What is Paul's attitude when facing possible death (verses 20-26), and why? Would we respond in the same way and, if not, why not?

9. What principles can we learn from verses 27-30 about how to handle persecution for our faith?

Chapter Two

1. Make a list, in your own words, of the things that Paul appeals to in verses 1-4 to encourage unity in the church.

2. In verse 5, Paul wants us to have an attitude which is *the same as that of Christ Jesus.* Read verses 6-11 and sum up that attitude in one sentence. How is such a mindset possible?

3. How does Jesus' approach contradict what we would normally expect of a great hero? And what does his attitude tell us about the way that God achieves things?

4. What truths are there in verses 6-11 that point to Jesus being unique among the founders of world religions?

5. Read verses 12 and 13. Do we live a 'good' Christian life because we work at it or because God helps us to do it? How does this work out in practice?

6. In the light of verses 14-16, how would you describe the Christian's relationship with society in general, and his/her responsibility towards it?

7. What do verses 19-24 reveal about Paul's thoughts and feelings towards the churches under his care, and those he worked with (compare 4:1)? Is there guidance here about how to choose and train leaders in the twenty-first century church?

8. What do verses 25-30 teach us about how to encourage and affirm each other?

9. Look at Philippians 1:21 and 2:21. Be honest, which verse best describes your life? Explain your answer.

Chapter Three

1. Who were those *mutilators of the flesh* that Paul wrote of in verses 2-4a, and why was he so angry towards them? Under what circumstances, if any, is it right for us to be angry like this?

2. In verses 4b-7, where do you get your sense of security from? Why is *confidence* through what we are in Christ much better?

3. How should your relationship with Christ determine your relationship to things? Try to think of some examples where being a Christian has actually changed your attitude towards possessions.

4. Verse 10 seems to suggest a link between suffering and power. Why might that be so? And what sort of power should we be seeking, and for what purpose?

5. Share some of the things that help you to *press on* (verse 12).

6. How does verse 13 help us deal with failure?

7. Does the *pattern* of life that Paul gives in verse 17 apply to all people in all ages? What would you say to someone who said we have outgrown this pattern and can experiment with new patterns? Illustrate from real life!

8. What point was Paul trying to make in verse 20 by saying that we are *citizens of heaven*? How should being this kind of citizen affect your behaviour as a citizen on earth?

9. What difference does it make to our everyday lives knowing that Jesus is coming back? And what does the fact that our ideal future involves a glorified *body* tell us about the value of physical things?

Chapter Four

1. We know from Paul's comment in verse 2 that the church at Philippi was not perfect. How do verses 2 and 3 help us deal with disagreements between Christians today?

2. According to verse 4 rejoicing is not first of all something we feel but something we do. What are some of the things all of us can do to *rejoice in the Lord*?

3. Is it always wrong to worry? Can anything beneficial come from worrying? Using verses 6 and 7, how would you try to help someone who was suffering from anxiety?

4. Why does Paul encourage us in verse 8 to *think* about certain things (and by implication not to think about other things)? What difference does it make in your life?

5. What can we learn from verses 10-20 about giving and receiving practical support to and from fellow Christians? What are some of the ways this could work out in your church?

6. What is the secret of *being content in any and every situation* (verse 12)? How can we learn to be content?

7. If God *will meet all your needs* (verse 19) why, apparently, are some of our needs not met? How do you explain Christians that have unmet needs for food, clothing, or shelter?

8. What does it mean in practical everyday living that *the grace of the Lord Jesus* is *with your spirit* (verse 23)?

9. What is the most important thing you have learned from this book? How will your life be different because of what you have learned?

TRANS WORLD RADIO
where hearing is believing

- 1.5 million listener letters per year
- responses from 160 different countries
- aired in 185 different languages and dialects
- more than 1,800 hours of programming each week

'THEIR VOICE GOES OUT INTO ALL THE EARTH,
THEIR WORDS TO THE ENDS OF THE WORLD.'
(Psalm 19:4)

- a biblical ministry
- a multimedia ministry
- a faith ministry
- a global ministry

THAT'S RADIO . . . TRANS WORLD RADIO!

For further information write to:

Trans World Radio	Trans World Radio	Trans World Radio
Southstoke Lane	P.O. Box 8700	P.O. Box 310
BATH	Cary	London
BA2 5SH	NC 27512	Ontario N6A 4W1
United Kingdom	USA	Canada